Family Traditions
for a
Fast-Paced World

Family Traditions for a Fast-Paced World:
Simple Everyday Rituals for Comfort and Connection
by Jordan St. Clair-Jackson (editor)

For information, contact Amberwood Press, Amberwoodinc@mac.com

Family Traditions for a Fast-Paced World

Simple Everyday Rituals for Comfort and Connection

Arranged and edited by Jordan St. Clair-Jackson

Contents

Introduction

Why Families Need Traditions in a Fast-Paced World

"Tradition is family insurance against outside pressures that threaten to overwhelm our days and weaken our ties to one another. We do not have to invest energy and time deciding what to do. We know what to do. With the weight of permanence and force of habit, tradition demands our attention."

— Susan Abel Lieberman, *New Traditions*

In these fast-paced times, many of us hunger for meaningful traditions we can pass on to our children, as well as share with family and friends. These don't have to be religious or cultural rites, or even things we recall from our own childhoods, but rather, little ways to embellish daily routines, create unique celebrations, and encourage fun activities that reflect our values and passions. Parents want to show love and affection to their children with actions as well as words. Your personal family rituals are the perfect way to do all of this and more. Conscious habits become beloved rituals; and rituals, repeated and enhanced over time, become traditions.

In our culture and others, among the most widely observed rituals relate to life cycle passages—births, birthdays, weddings, and the like. These and familiar holiday rites may be the only rituals many of us acknowledge. One of the simplest definitions of ritual, though, is right in the dictionary: Any customarily repeated act or series of acts. To this I would add, done with intention and creativity. It is these kinds of ordinary rituals that will be explored in this book—small, everyday ceremonies and personal traditions that can smooth life's rough edges, and add order and texture to the complex, busy lives of families.

The repetitive, cyclical, and predictable nature of rituals is what makes them comforting and reassuring. For families, establishing daily, monthly, and annual rituals creates lasting memories and powerful bonds. Everyday rituals need not be elaborate to be meaningful. On the contrary, the simpler, the better—aren't our lives complicated enough? Personal rituals can be an antidote to the relentless busy-ness and complexity of life.

For instance, by committing to an unwavering time each night to cuddle up and read aloud to a child, you create an unspoken promise, which kept regularly, conveys to your child that he or she comes first, and that this time shared over books is important. Adding sensual elements—a cozy comforter, a warm beverage to sip, a soft light—heightens the sensory experience. This is how a familiar ritual can produce a slowed-down, in-the-moment experience that becomes extraordinary in a quiet way.

Everyday rituals that were givens not long ago are now charming anachronisms. The family dinner, one of the most basic and nourishing of daily routines, has given way to after-school sports, lessons, late meetings, long commutes, and conflicting schedules.

Instead of making life simpler, technological devices and a glut of media have made it seem fragmented. Writing letters has been overtaken by e-mail and texting. Pop culture has supplanted more enriching forms of entertainment. Merely making time for reading a great book or getting together regularly with friends can seem like impossible dreams for busy parents.

Creating rituals around activities that give pleasure, but which we often find little time for, helps ensure that they will be part of our lives—whether interacting with good friends, enjoying meaningful family time, observing seasonal changes, reading, reflecting, or eating well. For example, we all need to eat every day. But too often, at the end of a tiring day, it's all too easy to rush highly processed or take-out meals to the table or rely on take-out. Within these pages you'll find plentiful inspiration for restoring the kitchen to its rightful place at the heart of the home, and learn how to create rituals for the daily dinner and special meals.

. . . . .

Routine vs. ritual — a matter of intent

Meg Cox, author of *The Heart of a Family,* so aptly puts it, "ritual is routine with sprinkles and hot sauce." A routine is something you do regularly because you need to, rather than because you choose to: You see your friends only when your frantic schedule allows; you nag your kids to get into bed; you rush up and down the aisles of the supermarket; you pile the kids into the car on Wednesdays to go to soccer practice.

Here are the intentional counterparts to dull routine: You participate in a monthly knitting or book group to connect with friends; you tell a story and sing two songs to your kids at bedtime; you stop at a produce market and an Italian grocery each Friday afternoon to get ingredients for an easy, festive end-of-the-week meal; you pile the kids into the car one Sunday each month for a special nature outing. The difference is that the latter group of actions are deliberate, and can be infused with personal touches that inspire anticipation.

In this book you'll be invited both to rediscover the role ritual can play in daily family life, and how personal traditions can bring order to lives that can sometimes feel chaotic. In this sometimes uncomfortable era, it should come as little surprise that quite a few women find comfort in rituals that recall simpler times, such as picking produce to bake into pies, canning jam and tomatoes, or participating in knitting circles.

On the other hand, we may not be able to gather for the Norman Rockwell-style Sunday supper at Grandma's, if she lives three thousand miles away or prefers skiing in the Rockies to spending all day over a hot stove. But if we long for a sense of connection over food, we can participate in a regular Sunday potluck with local family members, or a monthly dinner club with friends.

Though I welcome male readers to these pages, you'll note that it is written from the female perspective; all the stories and most of the quotes are from female voices. This is by no means meant to be exclusionary; though men certainly enjoy participating in rituals, I simply found that women are far more often the ones who initiate and maintain rituals in family life and among their friends. You'll find many delightful stories of how women have tailored rituals to suit the needs of contemporary family life. Use these and the many simple ideas in these pages as a springboard to developing rituals and traditions suited to your family's needs.

It's worth taking the time to think about what everyday traditions you might have cherished as a child, and how you can pass these along to your own children. Apart from the big holiday traditions that may immediately leap to mind, recall those activities that gave you a sense of continuity and security when you were younger—the annual road trip, barbecues on the beach, weekly dinner with the grandparents, moonlit walks with your dad. Granted, for those of us who had less-than-idyllic childhoods, what's past may be best left there. If that's the case for you, give yourself the gift of an expansive blank canvas on which to create new traditions and rituals from scratch for your family and friends.

In these rapidly changing, increasingly impersonal times, everyday traditions and simple rituals can help shape and order our experiences as individuals and as a family unit. They allow us to relish and appreciate the present, rather than rushing toward whatever we think we need to do next. Incorporating rituals into daily life requires a shift in attitude and tiny sparks of inspiration rather than sizable chunks of time.

By transforming our already existing patterns and fundamental pleasures into satisfying rituals and simple ceremonies, we can cement and expand the blessings already present in our lives and more readily enhance the lives of those to whom we're connected.

What is a modern family, and who is this book for?

Let's be clear here. Though I grew up in a fairly "traditional" family — that is, married parents with kids in a nuclear arrangement, and then repeated that pattern myself, that's not what necessarily constitutes a family. What makes a family is however you define it, and what you create.

Married or unmarried; mom and dad and kids; two moms or two dads and kids; single parents; blended families; multi-generational families; grandparents raising their grandchildren; families with adopted or foster children. Two partners without children also constitute a family, of course, though this book is geared primarily toward families with kids. If I've forgotten anything in that list, it's unintentional! And if the language in this book is more specific than general, please gear it to your personal situation.

The interviewees for this book were mainly women. Of course, men have been playing a greater role in parenting, but as I explored this subject, I found that women (where two opposite-sex partners are involved) are still by and large the keepers of the family schedule, activities, and traditions. Though this is slowly changing, I hope you'll see beyond the female perspective in these pages and see that these ideas can be used by anyone.

The modern family might look many different ways, but we all have similar aspirations for our children, at the top of which are safe, secure, and enriching upbringings.

What inspired this book

Like many busy parents, I'm guilty of having given little thought to my family's traditions and rituals when my kids were small. My husband and I weren't youngsters when we plunged into parenthood. We began this journey with little role modeling, having grown up, like many of our generation, in families whose ideas about parenting were fundamentally different from ours. Who had time to think about rituals? The notion never even occurred to me, though now, of course, I wish it had.

A few winters ago, we unexpectedly found ourselves rather under-scheduled. Soccer season was over, an interest in piano lessons had waned, and a long winter break loomed with no vacation plans. Once conscious of this, the four of us (my husband and I and our two sons, then in the later elementary school years) mutually agreed to make the experience more deliberate. Extracurricular activities and sports were put on hold; we ate out and went to the movies only occasionally. We did continue to see extended family and friends, though bowing to winter hibernation, not as frequently as during other times of the year.

I began to explore how I could incorporate simpler activities and pleasures into our family life. The results were more gratifying than I ever could have anticipated, and from this brief interlude, several cherished rituals emerged. Reading aloud to my sons was already a beloved family ritual, but with more time on our hands, it became a passion.

For a brief but intensive time, we delved into classic fairy tales and ethnic folktales. From there, we immersed ourselves in the giddily bizarre world of Roald Dahl. Then, our read-aloud ritual continued with a focus on children's classics, including *Peter Pan, Alice in Wonderland and Through the Looking Glass,* and *Tom Sawyer.*

A longtime winter-hater, I grew fonder of the season, thanks to all the comforts we established or cemented that year. We put out a backyard bird feeder for wintering birds, and were amazed at the variety that came along. A bird book provided a fun way to identify our feathered visitors, and the kids videotaped each variety.

Getting snowshoes provided an incentive for walking in the snow (I was actually disappointed that we had so little snow the winter following). Of course, coming in and sitting by the fire with tea or cocoa afterwards is what makes snowshoeing more of a winter ritual than a sport. We also initiated a tradition of buying a large jigsaw puzzle at the beginning of each winter to work on slowly throughout the season, especially during snow days.

An interest in baking homemade quick breads, cookies, and muffins flourished that year. My younger son was nearly always in the kitchen with me, and together, we developed a repertoire of delicious and healthy baked goods. Baking with my younger son became a favorite ritual for stormy days. By the age of eleven, he became an accomplished baker in his own right. Though we have never since been as under-scheduled as we were that one wonderful winter, many of the traditions we established then have carried forward into each successive winter.

Rituals and traditions—why they're great for families
Discovering the joys of ritual and tradition when we had a bit more free and open time didn't make me feel like any sort of expert. On the contrary, it made me feel sad that this discovery didn't happen until my children were well out of early childhood.

That said, it's never too late to initiate rituals. Even teens can benefit greatly from family traditions, and given the right cues, can be of great help in initiating and maintaining them. My curiosity led me to explore the subject further, talking to friends about their own rituals and traditions.

William J. Doherty, Ph.D., points out in *The Intentional Family* that rituals enhance many of those activities that you already engage in: "You have to feed your children, so start with improving the quality of those feeding rituals, without lengthening the time. You have to put your kids to bed; work on making it more pleasurable. You probably have birthday parties, holiday celebrations, and countless family activities." Exploring the possibilities for enhancing these ordinary activities makes a world of difference when we distinguish routine from ritual.

> *"The security aspect of ritual and repetition is more significant in the current age than ever before. For families who move constantly or who endure divorce and remarriage, job insecurity, and all the constant unknowns, rituals are comforting simply because they are one of the few things over which families still have control."*
>
> — Meg Cox, *The Heart of a Family*

- ***Rituals help give order and rhythm to a child's day.*** Parenting experts agree that the predictability and repetition of daily rituals makes for more secure children. Family dinner, the walk to school, a young child's bath, bedtime stories—these common rituals, if not particularly original or exciting, convey to a child that even the simplest of daily activities can be times for comfort and connection.

- ***Rituals help ease daily transitions.*** The transition from wakefulness to sleep, for example, is especially challenging for young children and their exhausted parents; special rituals make going to bed fun, rather than stressful. The daily transition of parting can be made less daunting with a group hug, special handshakes, or secret signals.

- ***Rituals give families various ways to express love.*** These can include how you greet one another in the morning, or how you say good night; how you care for one another when someone is sick or has had a difficult day; the unique ways you show appreciation for each member of the family; or simply the ways and frequency with which you verbalize "I love you." Though many of us practice daily rituals without being conscious of them, they are more delightful when deliberate.

- ***Rituals reinforce tradition.*** Whether part of a larger framework (such as faith or community) or personal to the individual family, traditions—as long as they remain meaningful and pleasurable and not rote or obligatory—are the footprint of each family's history. They gently recall the past while rooting us in the present.

- ***Traditions link generations.*** Carrying traditions forward helps children feel more connected to their extended family. Maybe you bake the same cookies that your mother and grandmother did; or you celebrate a grandparent's birthday by gathering and telling well-worn but beloved family stories each year. Perhaps you pull out an old family photo album on a particular anniversary or birthday. Any such simple rituals can be an enchanting link to the past.

- *Everyday rituals express family values without judgment or preaching.* A family that loves the arts can set up monthly outings to art museums, and decide in advance on interesting activities to do while there. Parents who cherish nature can introduce their children to special places to explore and revisit each season. Families who wish to teach the value of giving can create rituals around volunteering and donating.

It's best to remain flexible where family rituals are concerned. As your children grow, they may no longer need a bedtime story, but might still appreciate having you sit with them for a quiet chat or a back rub at bedtime. Some rituals dwindle naturally, while others evolve into something new. Others remain firmly rooted as kids grow older. If a ritual begins meeting with resistance, it's time to let go; once it feels forced, it's no more fun than any other obligation.

My own discovery of everyday traditions and ordinary rituals grew from the unexpected gift of more open time. But I believe that awareness is more crucial than great swathes of time for recognizing and finding regular time for them in the course of any busy life. They don't add to your "to-do" list, but rather, give you a sense that more time is being created in the midst of your busy life. By deciding what's important, creating little pockets of time becomes surprisingly easy.

It's stating the obvious that many kids today are over-scheduled, rushed, and sometimes stressed by too much activity. And the cultural addiction to screen time doesn't help matters. Rituals create islands of calm and predictability, perfect antidotes to overstuffed schedules. We don't need more "downtime" in order to create rituals; rather, rituals actually become the downtime we all crave, whether it's sharing stories each night, having a pizza-and-movie night once a week, hiking alongside a waterfall each spring, or enjoying a memorable birthday celebration every year.

Family rituals and traditions are the simplest yet strongest forms of connection and comfort for all involved, and can undoubtedly be the basis of our children's fondest memories.

"Rituals are repeated patterns of meaningful acts. If you are mindful of your actions, you will see the ritual patterns. If you see the patterns, you may understand them. If you understand them, you may enrich them. In this way, the habits of a lifetime become sacred."

— Robert Fulghum, *From Beginning to End*

Part One
In the Kitchen
and at the Table

"One of the primary ways we connect with each other is by eating together . . . Much of our fundamental well-being comes from the basic reassurance that there is a place for us at the table. We belong here. Here we are served and we serve others. Here we give and receive sustenance. No small matter."

—Edward Espe Brown,
Tomato Blessings and Radish Teachings

Family Dinner at the Table: Reconsidering an Endangered Ritual

Cooking and eating offer abundant opportunities to bring rituals of comfort and pleasure into daily life, simply because we all need to eat every day. Yet, often, they're missed opportunities, as frozen entrées, makeshift meals, and take-out menus call to our craving for convenience. No wonder so many Western cultures have become overfed and undernourished. Serving fresh food that's been prepared with love (or at least a good attitude) and seasoned with camaraderie is a simple formula for nourishing both body and spirit on a daily basis.

With work schedules, lessons, and sports practices pulling family members in all directions just as the day should be winding down, it's no wonder fewer families are finding the time to eat together. Yet, at the same time, it's encouraging to know that many others are making a great effort to keep this ritual alive.

Studies have been done comparing children and teens who have regular family dinners at home with those who don't. The results are consistent, and striking. Teens from families who eat dinner together are less likely to use illegal drugs, alcohol, and cigarettes than teenagers who rarely eat dinner with their parents. Another practical (if predictable) perk is that children who have regular, at-home dinners eat meals that are healthier and include more vegetables.

In addition, children who have regular family dinners are believed to fare better in school. Few daily rituals offer better opportunity to connect, converse, share, and feel nourished.

What's on the table and how it's presented speaks volumes about our willingness to give mealtime rituals the place they so richly deserve in daily life. Don't buy into the myth that it's too time consuming to put a decent dinner on the table regularly. Still, meals aren't only about the food on the table. The setting, atmosphere, stories, and conversations that accompany the food all contribute to making even the most ordinary meal memorable. Consider:

- Is your kitchen the heart of the home, or the center of the cyclone? Because of its central location in most homes and apartments, kitchens often become repositories for mail, bills, school notices, homework, recent purchases, newspapers, unfinished projects, toys, and more. Make sure your kitchen suggests food and comfort, not clutter and chaos. It's more the attitude one brings to the kitchen than its decor that matters; it can become, to some degree, a sacred space.

  "Thinking of your kitchen as a temple may be just what you need to bring more harmony into your life," suggest Robin Robertson and Jon Robertson, authors of *The Sacred Kitchen*. The kitchen should be comfortable, functional, and as clutter-free as possible. Give it some sensuous elements, plus some hint of the season.

- Do your shopping habits contribute positively or negatively to your attitude toward meal preparation? Do you plan your meals and pantry needs so that shopping can be at least a pleasant, if not downright enjoyable routine? Does your food shopping include planned stops at farm stands and organic produce markets, quality bakeries, and ethnic food shops?

  If you find yourself frantically prowling the aisles of crowded supermarkets without a list in hand, or if you wait until there is literally nothing in the house with which to make a simple meal, you need to rethink your shopping habits.

• If your meals are primarily shared with a partner, how do the two of you make them significant? Are you using them as a time to connect after a busy day and catch up with one another, or do you chow down over the mail or evening news? Couples who spend long days apart might consider how they can create regular mealtimes that aren't merely a time to eat, but a way to reconnect.

• Do you bond over food regularly with extended family and/or friends? Plenty of families still hold to the tradition of a weekly Sabbath meal (the Friday night Shabbat dinner of the Jewish faith, the after-church Sunday dinner practiced by many Christians). Yet others enjoy regular extended family meals as a matter of course, without the structure of faith.

Casting a wide net of family connection with food as the common denominator is one of the most time-honored ways to connect, and an ideal way to have cousins grow up together, to see aunts and uncles, siblings, and grandparents without having to make separate plans.

• Amy's grandparents, Italian immigrants who settled in the New York City suburbs (with four offspring), retained certain cultural values that kept their family together, while in other ways assimilating. A Friday night pizza dinner (with every part of the pizza made from scratch by Amy's grandmother) has been, as Amy puts it, "a family institution."

When Amy was growing up, it was a way to play with cousins and visit with aunts and uncles. As a teen, she sometimes resented having to participate, but now, as a young woman, she claims she wouldn't miss this gathering for the world. And the homemade pizza is a must. Once, her grandmother decided to skip the pizza and serve turkey, which sent the family into shock! That never happened again.

- Finally, have you begun any food traditions for your children that will foster warm memories and a healthy relationship with food for your children as they grow up? Hopefully, they won't leave home only with recollections of the take-out menu drawer and cereal cabinet!

"Of all the rooms in our lives, the kitchen can feed the soul and become a comforting place to be at any time of day. I think of the kitchen as a gathering place, a place for shared comforts, for mutual efforts at preparing good meals with loving care.

— Alexandra Stoddard, *Living a Beautiful Life*

Making the Table a Welcoming Place

Set the table, set the tone: It takes little effort to make the table look welcoming with dishes and utensils that you and your family enjoy using. This may not seem like a major point, but like the three bowls used at Buddhist monasteries, they are an intrinsic part of the experience. The tableware you use should be both functional and interesting: ceramic dishes that lend an earthy flair to the table, jazzy colorful plates, or vintage dishes that belonged to your grandmother.

Maybe your little ones can have their own special plates—small, colorful dishes might help them enjoy the dinner ritual that much more. Some families use certain dishes or a special candlestick only when all are able to be present at the table. Fresh flowers, a seasonal centerpiece, colorful napkins—all these little touches help bring attention to what is before us. From a young age, children can set the dinner table. Allow them some creative freedom, within reason, and encourage them to include personal and seasonal touches. A little whimsy adds to the spirit of a shared meal.

Have a beginning and ending: A signal that the meal is about to begin, such as lighting candles or reciting a blessing, helps create a framework for the experience. Teach your kids to respect the cook by waiting to take the first bite until he or she is seated. As soon as it's realistic to do so, get children into the habit of sitting through the meal until everyone is done, but be flexible. Better to let your little ones go off and play rather than get restless at the table; likewise, if your adolescents are inundated with schoolwork, don't require them to sit for undue time at the table. The end of the meal can be signaled by thanking the cook and cleaning up together. Make sure that everyone participates in cleanup; those who left the table earlier should come back and pitch in.

Engage the senses: Rounding up the family and putting a nourishing meal on the table daily is challenging enough, to be sure. But once you establish a comfortable routine, you can begin to transform dinner from routine to ritual. By engaging the senses, even ordinary meals can be memorable. The beauty of candles or flowers at the table, the snap and crunch of a raw vegetable platter, the surprising flavor of a fruit salsa or chutney on the plate, the scent of fresh bread, the touch of hands joined around the table for a moment of gratitude—these are but a few ways to add to the pleasure of eating with a few easy nods to the senses.

Sit and chat: Ideally, of course, the dinner table should be a place for conversation and connection. The reality is that by the time we sit down to the evening meal, many of us (especially if younger children are involved) feel too weary for sparkling repartee. And the tendency to watch something on TV or look at one's electronic devices doesn't make matters easier. It helps to provide a common thread from day to day, such as going around the table and having everyone talk about the highlight of their day. Dinnertime is for checking in, exchanging news, and enjoying good food and one another's company.

Having a set of prompts in mind works well to spark conversation. Discuss an interesting news story or community event, or have everyone talk about the high point of their day. You can occasionally celebrate or commemorate something that happened on that date — a significant historic event, or the birthday of a person we admire. If you want to keep conversation light, try "conversation-in-a-jar," suggested by Meg Cox in *The Book of New Family Traditions*. Prepare a container to be set on the table, containing strips of paper marked with open-ended statements such as "The strangest thing that happened to me today was . . ."

Explore blessings: Many families enjoy starting the meal with some sort of blessing; others find this feels rather awkward. Some report that saying a blessing can at first feel forced, but after a while, it becomes a calming way to begin a meal.

If you'd like to explore this idea in a less conventional way, consider going outside your personal tradition with blessings from other cultures. Chinese, Indian, Native American, Tibetan, Irish, and others have lovely blessings that can be adopted—or adapted! A few lines from a favorite poem can also be an offbeat way to open your meal. *Saying Grace: Blessings for the Family Table* (edited by Sarah McElwain) is a little book filled with ideas from world religious traditions, great poets, Aesop, and even cowboys.

Carlie's family eats dinner together each day gives thanks for our food, saying the same prayer each time, with each person saying their little bit. "Then we go around again, and each adds a personal entry," she says, "giving thanks for something positive that affected us during the day — anything from seeing the sun or having a friend over, to getting some work done, or having a good day at school."

Be flexible and realistic: If your family's schedule simply won't allow for dinner at the table every night, try to carve out the time for at least some meals together. If it's only twice a week, so be it; make the most of those meals together. Families of all denominations appoint the Sabbath as the regular meal to come together for, and this creates a lovely container for this ritual.

In truth, it's unrealistic to expect relaxing family meals with toddlers, babies, and tired young children. Up until they were school age, I often fed my kids dinner early so that my husband and I could enjoy a quiet meal. We kept revisiting the concept of eating as a family at regular intervals as they grew up. Gradually, a full-fledged family dinner evolved. Generally, kids are ready for the dinner ritual once they are school age. Remember, rigid food rituals are hardly better than no rituals at all.

Candles at the table: Candles are often saved for special occasions, though their soothing glow provides an easy way to elevate the nightly meal. The simple act of lighting candles gives the meal a definite beginning; older children enjoy this task. Dinner is over when the candles are blown out—the perfect "job" for little ones.

Candles are most welcome during the dark days of the year. For casual daily meals, try short, chunky candles or colorful tapers in ceramic holders. It's also fun to set a tiny tea light at everyone's place. Send a long, safe candle around so everyone can light their individual candle. When the meal is over, everyone blows out their own candle. While hardly a revolutionary idea, candles can sharpen the focus of a family dinner, while softening the atmosphere.

When Barbara's sons were growing up, her family practiced a candle-lighting ceremony at the dinner table each night. Each member of the family took a turn at lighting the dinner candle, dedicating it to whatever they wished, for example, to a grandparent or even a cherished cause.

"It gave us a chance to combine giving, loving thoughts, and an action," Barbara recalled. "This ceremony becomes a wonderfully potent and useful structure within which we can express feelings, thoughts, desires, and dreams that add a new level of communication and sharing. The beauty of the candles alone seems to engender beautiful and sacred thoughts and expressions, and have a positive transformational effect on any negative moods that we may have developed from the stresses of the day."

. . . . .

Cooking Together

In *A Bite Off Mama's Plate: Mothers' and Daughters' Connections Through Food*, Miriam Meyers portrays the kitchen as a feminine world of activity and communication. Whether the stories of mothers and daughters in the kitchen take place in the past or present (helping, learning, or often just talking as Mom cooked, baked, and canned), they carry an air of nostalgia. One woman describes the fun of helping with the weekly baking of pies, donuts, and breads with her mother and grandmother on Saturday mornings.

I would have thought this activity somewhat of a relic, had I not personally met a mother and her two twenty-something daughters who bake and cook together on Saturdays, not out of necessity, but as a pleasurable ritual.

Cooking together has gone beyond the traditional paradigm of daughters learning at their mothers' apron strings, and fortunately, is no longer limited to the females in the family. Some families have developed rituals for cooking as a team, whether for daily dinner or for fun and relaxation, often with male partners and sons as equal participants. Sometimes, the daily necessity of getting a meal on the table can feel like a lonely task when it is the domain of just one cook. When you involve your partner or children in the process of creating meals, you also create a perfect opportunity to pass down food customs and share culinary passions.

When little ones are in the picture, many harried parents feel that they need to somehow keep them busy and out from underfoot while they throw together a quick meal. Jennifer, however, had her kids cook with her from the time they were young. When her son was very small, she got him a play stove and allowed him to "cook" using safe utensils. After her daughter came along and the kids got older, she gave them age-appropriate tasks to help prepare the meal. Jennifer admits that having her children cook with her made the process a little messier and lengthier, but they got the message that she was completely present with them.

Even if you don't cook meals with your family every day, sharing some cooking activities helps create memorable comfort food rituals. Baking is a perfect kitchen activity to share with kids, since the steps are relatively easy, and the results are delectable. This skill can be passed along to your children from a very early age and developed into a shared pastime.

For Peggy, baking with her daughters, Katherine and Annie, has long been a shared passion that continues as the girls have become young women. At twenty, Katherine, her younger daughter, can hardly remember a time when she didn't bake with her mother and older sister. All of seven years old when she attempted her first solo baking venture, the jelly roll cake she made for family breakfast was a complete success.

After Annie left for college, school breaks meant coming

home and spending time in the kitchen with her mother and sister, especially for holiday and special occasion meals. Now, post-college and living on her own, many Saturdays still find Annie visiting home, continuing the tradition of baking and cooking as a trio. Mornings are for baking something sweet yet healthful together, like banana-nut bread or carrot cake. After the baking is done, the three decide what they want to make for dinner. Sometimes they pore over cookbooks, make lists, and shop for ingredients; other times, they shop first and improvise later. Either way, the entire process is pleasurable and relaxing.

To hear Katherine tell it, the common bond of cooking something delicious and innovative that is suitable for their meatless diet is surpassed only by how happy they are to be in the kitchen together. Their delectable dishes are shared with their father and their teenage brother, who, though not completely in tune with the healthy food philosophy of the women in the family, are beginning to come around. Whether making meals together, or cooking recreationally, lessons learned around the kitchen counter last a lifetime.

Resources
Cooking Time Is Family Time: Cooking Together, Eating Together, and Spending Time Together by Lynn Fredericks is all about the art of cooking and eating together as a family.

Honest Pretzels: And 64 Other Amazing Recipes for Kids Ages 8 and Up by Mollie Katzen. Here's one of the best books around for budding chefs who want to cook independently for their families.

The Family Dinner: Great Ways to Connect with Your Kids, One Meal at a Time by Laurie David. The film producer's mission is to help America's overwhelmed families sit down to family dinner, and she provides all the reasons, recipes, and fun tools to help achieve that goal.

Dinner, a Love Story by Jenny Rosenstrach. A combination memoir, practical how-to guide, and cookbook, this book had many tips for strengthening family bonds by making the most of dinnertime.

Dinner Club with Family and Friends

After a busy week, few but the most diehard foodies enjoy the added stress of planning, cooking, and serving a grand meal to a small crowd, especially if it's not any special occasion or holiday. Still, dinner parties are fun, and the desire to host and participate in them lingers on.

As formal dinner parties diminish, the trend toward potluck gatherings has grown. Potlucks are an ideal way to spend time and share food with friends and family. When each participant needs to prepare only one dish, they'll often pull out all the stops and make something truly delicious and creative.

When potlucks become a regular event shared by a given group of friends or several families, they are transformed into what is now known as a "dinner club." Dinner clubs are the new incarnation of the once-in-a-while, random potluck, transformed into a richly rewarding ritual to share with friends. They're a great way to test out and share ideas for healthy plant-based meals. Some dinner clubs encourage participants to share recipes by printing up enough copies for everyone to take home.

Here are tips for starting and maintaining a successful dinner club. How do you decide on who participates in a dinner club? The most obvious answer is to glean a few other couples or families who you would like to socialize with on a regular basis. Having set, planned dates helps ensure that you gather over a shared interest in great food and camaraderie. Here are some nuts and bolts questions to ask yourself as you get a club up and running:

- Will the club be made up of families, couples only, or just women, as a way to get some "girlfriend time"?

- Should the meal be served buffet or family style?

- Should the club rotate among all members' homes, or just those that have ample space?

- Will members bring dishes that are entirely made, or will the participants cook at least some of the meal together?

- How will you handle non-food details, like beverages, plates, napkins and utensils?

- How will you decide on themes and menus? Will budget be a consideration in planning meals? A few other tips to get you started:

Consider compassion: Some clubs set aside a portion of the food, and make plates of extra food to bring to someone elderly or ill in the neighborhood. Others take up a modest collection of cash, or ask participants to bring some good quality nonperishable food to donate to a local food bank or soup kitchen.

Pull focus: Some dinner clubs are more focused than random potlucks. Whoever is hosting can decide on a theme, then coordinate via e-mail. The components of the meal can be assigned, or volunteered for. It's also best to have set dates in place, such as the last Sunday of even-number months, rather than trying to figure out each time what is going to work for everyone.

If you want to go beyond the moment of sharing and savoring, ask everyone to bring enough copies of their recipe to share with the other participants. Guests can also bring empty storage containers for sharing leftovers. Here are some themes to ponder:

Comfort food: Winter months are a perfect time for a comfort food theme. After the excesses of the holidays, participants will appreciate simple, homespun dishes. Have everyone bring not only their favorite comfort food, but the story behind it.

Global: Mexican, Italian, Thai, Middle Eastern, and Japanese are perennial favorites; it's less daunting to prepare one dish from a favorite cuisine than a whole meal. Use a favorite cookbook or two to create an ethnic menu to parcel out among participants.

Soup and stew sampler: Have three or four participants bring a medium-sized pot of their favorite soup or stew and a ladle. Others can provide fresh bread, tossed salad, and dessert.

Celebrate special occasions: This is especially fun for nondenominational holidays that you might otherwise skip celebrating. Valentine's Day, St. Patrick's Day, Cinco de Mayo, and other holidays lend themselves to festive culinary themes.

. . . .

Pack a picnic: If possible, have your dinner club enjoy at least one meal per year picnic-style at a beautiful outdoor venue.

Comfort Foods: Soothing Traditions

From an infant's first sip of milk, the connection between sustenance and security is forged. Comfort food is the edible equivalent of a security blanket—soothing and delightfully childish. Often bland, soft, creamy, warm, meltingly sweet, or even mushy, comfort food can calm and console before taking a single bite.

If you're a bit blue or under the weather, complex flavors that ordinarily delight may not be just what you need. A dollop of mashed potatoes or a bowl of noodle soup might do your spirit more good than any spicy delicacy seasoned with cilantro, garlic, or jalapeño peppers.

And let's be perfectly clear—food as a comfort is not the same as food as a fix. Downing an entire bag of oily, salty chips or box of cookies doesn't equal the conscious savoring of "nursery foods" that trigger nostalgic connections to special people and simpler times. Comfort food is a respite, not a compulsion.

While the all-American definition of comfort food is fairly universal (macaroni and cheese; rice pudding; soups and stews; cookies, brownies, and pies; fresh muffins and biscuits; mashed potatoes, pot pie, stuffing, and other "grandma" food), in reality it's quirkier, more personal, and reflects one's ethnic roots. Few of us, regardless of current food preferences, waxes nostalgic about big bowls of steamed broccoli or raw salads.

· ·

*"A long time ago it occurred to me that when people are
tired and hungry, which in adult life is much of the time,
they do not want to be confronted by an intellectually
challenging meal: they want to be consoled. When life is
hard and the day has been long, the ideal dinner is not
four perfect courses . . . but rather something comforting and savory, easy on the digestion—something that
makes one feel, if even for only a minute,
that one is safe."*

— Laurie Colwin, *Home Cooking*

For everyone who regaled me with a great comfort food memory,
another drew a blank, myself included. Having rebelled against
my childhood foods, my notions seem to have been drawn from
memories of perfect 1950s TV moms — June Cleaver serving
freshly baked cookies to "The Beaver" after school, Donna Reed
swirling gracefully into the dining room with fluffy mashed potatoes. But having no such traditions from my past has inspired
me to create new ones for my children. You might consider doing so, too.

Creamy or noodle-filled soups, homemade macaroni and
cheese, and our beloved repertoire of wholesome baked goods
are among the comforts I've seen follow my kids into adulthood. I hope they'll also remember sitting on high stools in the
kitchen helping to stir batters, the scent of chocolate coming
from the oven, and having me read Calvin and Hobbes aloud as
they enjoyed freshly baked brownies.

The stories gathered here demonstrate how memory and
senses become entwined, conjuring up the comfort foods that

become part of our family history. The cozy food memories are most always connected with a special person (usually a parent or grandmother), and often, a ritual connected with the making or eating of the food.

- While growing up, Geetha's parents regularly made idli (steamed rice cakes, eaten plain or with butter and sugar) for her. A traditional Indian comfort food served for soothing major ailments and minor maladies, idli are also a cherished Sunday breakfast treat, much as pancakes are in Western kitchens.

  Geetha now makes idli for her young daughter, Indira, who enthusiastically eats them out of hand. Making them is no small project; they even require special cooking equipment. But, Geetha says, idli evoke such comforting memories that making them for her daughter "is just one of those things that, busy as I am, I've chosen to do anyway."

- Proving that personal notions of comfort food are unique, two sisters, Robin and Leah, grew up in the same house and ate the same bland Eastern European Jewish food. Robin never liked it, and today, as a raw food enthusiast, politely rebuffs her mother's cajoling. For Leah, on the other hand, returning home to matzo ball soup, sweet potato tzimmes, and noodle pudding (which she does about once a month) makes her feel as well cared for as when she was young and her biggest worry was which jumper to wear to school.

  "I never cook this way at home," says Robin, who favors salads and rice dishes, "but it's not just the food. It's about how in Mom's world, so little has changed—the rosebud wallpaper in the dining room, the doilies on the end tables, the aromas, and the friendly nagging to eat a just a little more when I'm ready to burst. It's a welcome relief from my stressful job."

- Karen loved visiting her Norwegian grandparents for Christmas in the Midwest as a child. Her grandmother always baked *kringlas* — a traditional pastry formed into a sort of figure eight, which Karen would wash down with cinnamon-scented hot cocoa. These were served with a special plate and cup set that were just for Karen's use when she came to visit.

  "They had bunnies around the rim — or were they kitties?" she mused. Though the recollection has grown fuzzy, she acknowledges that the plate and cup were crucial to the ritual. For years, Karen has baked several batches of *kringlas* during the holiday season to give as hostess gifts and to serve to guests. No bunny or kitty dishes are involved, but she does use her grandmother's original recipe.

- Olive learned to cook the old-fashioned way — at her mother's side, on the family farm near Montego Bay, Jamaica. Her mother grew everything the family needed for sustenance, from tangerines, bananas, coconuts, plantains, and avocados to coffee and cocoa beans. Each day, food was freshly picked and prepared.

  "On Sundays," she recalled, "we made 'rice and peas,' just like every family on the island does." The tasty national dish of Jamaica is made with rice, small dried red beans, a whole fresh coconut, and lots of onions and garlic. After

Olive moved to the United States, she so missed her home that she continues to make a big pot of rice and peas each Sunday, giving away portions of it to anyone who comes her way or whom she might be visiting.

Doing so, she says, keeps her connected to Jamaican cooking rituals, as well as to the memories of her long-departed mother and her kitchen.

"It seems to me that our three basic needs, for food and security and love, are so entwined that we cannot think of one without the other."

— M.F.K. Fisher

Breakfast comfort

Special breakfast traditions are rarely a lot of work, since they often revolve around just one food. Pancakes, waffles, biscuits, bagels, and fresh muffins seem tailor-made for enjoying in one's pajamas, reading the morning paper. A breakfast ritual can be the perfect antidote to the weekday morning "rush hour" or a special treat on weekends.

- Sunday mornings find Carlie's family around the table with a special breakfast that's not large or elaborate, but different from what they have during the week: "When we were on sabbatical in Cambridge for a year, I made what we call scones, not really English scones, but a kind of cinnamon biscuit, slightly sweet. At home, John makes waffles. We often have some fruit and tea, or coffee and juice. We all look forward to this simple Sunday morning meal—it's a nice way to start the week."

- Mary, who has two older school-age children, initiated a ritual that she calls "Thursday pancake day." When Mary was growing up, her mother made pancakes every Friday morning. She has always treasured a vivid recollection of how much fun it was, so she started to do the same for her kids. They, too, love it, but asked that she switch the day to Thursday, their hardest day at school. The pancake ritual gives them comforting sustenance for the day ahead.

- Gail grew up in a small southern town in the 1950s, where hers was the only Jewish family. Bagels and grits for breakfast became the odd yet apt metaphor for -preserving cultural identity while trying to fit in. When I asked her if she still eats bagels and grits, she said that this particular combination was strictly of that time and place. Grits are still a top choice for comfort, though. She serves grits and eggs or cheese grits to her family for breakfast on a regular basis.

Our daily bread

Bread is the original comfort food. Few experiences offer more pleasure than the earthy flavors and yeasty aromas of freshly baked bread. Every culture has a characteristic bread, little changed for generations, that's completely ingrained in daily life as well as cultural and religious rituals. Think of Middle Eastern pita bread; Indian naan, puri, and chapatis; Jewish challah; Mexican tortillas.

Gluten-free trends aside, there's a been a surge of interest in artisanal bread baking, utilizing traditional European methods, wood-fired ovens, and robust whole grains.

Baking bread at home can be a pleasurable ritual for those who are attracted to its earthy, tactile pleasures. It offers a hands-on way to center oneself, and can be a productive way to enjoy quiet time. Because it engages the senses and requires repetitive movement and some precision, many people who bake bread for pleasure find the process quite meditative.

When Martina received a bread machine from a couple of friends for her fortieth birthday, she thanked them kindly and exchanged it for a slow cooker. For her, the process of baking bread is just as important as the result. Without being involved in the rhythm of kneading, the feel of the dough, and the yeasty scents, she feels she may as well buy bread from the bakery in town.

Though Martina has two young daughters, her baking ritual helps her claim quiet time that's for herself alone. Since her family almost always spends Friday evenings at home, after dinner, her husband plays board games and reads with the girls. That's their special time with Dad, and Martina's special time to make dough for two large loaves of bread. She takes her time kneading two different batches of dough, finding the process relaxing and meditative; then she sets them in a barely warm oven to rise overnight.

Saturday mornings find Martina up very early. The dough is punched down and shaped into loaves, then she goes out for a run for the duration of the second rising. Once home, the bread is popped into the oven, and the rest of the family wakes to the smell of fresh bread, which is savored throughout the weekend. If any bread is left, it becomes part of Monday night's dinner, served with a soup or stew in her useful slow cooker.

. . . .

Bread makes itself, by your kindness, with your help, with imagination running through you, with dough under hand, you are breadmaking itself, which is why breadmaking is so fulfilling and rewarding.

— Edward Espe Brown, *The Tassajara Bread Book*

Resources

There are many excellent books on baking bread. Here are just a few:

Bread Alone: Bold Fresh Loaves from Your Own Hands by Daniel Leader and Judith Blahnick

The Tassajara Bread Book by Edward Espe Brown

Breadtime: A Down-to-Earth Cookbook for Bakers and Bread Lovers by Susan Jane Cheney

And to inspire kids, here are two books aimed at younger bakers and their parents:

Knead it, Punch it, Bake it! The Ultimate Breadmaking Book for Parents and Kids by Judith and Evan Jones

Loaves of Fun: A History of Bread with Activities and Recipes from Around the World by Elizabeth M. and John Harbison

Seasonal Food Pleasures

A growing movement has been encouraging people to use as many locally grown foods as possible. At a time when small farmers are struggling to survive, this helps local economies and is a more sustainable practice than continually buying food trucked into supermarkets over thousands of miles.

The call to use one local food per day has gotten me to thinking about how drastically my own shopping habits have changed over the last few years. I pick up my family's share of just-picked organic produce once a week from May through November at the CSA (Community Supported Agriculture) farm we belong to; I shop at a local natural foods store once or twice a week for fruits and veggies I can't get at the CSA, as well as other staples. In season, I visit local farm markets on a regular basis.

My new food-gathering habits have become pleasant rituals. I enjoy chatting with the growers and fellow members at the CSA. Supporting local businesses like the natural foods market feels better than traipsing the aisles of chain supermarkets. I always chat with the employees, and often sip a cup of organic coffee or freshly made juice while I shop. I don't really need to shop at farm markets, but that, too, is a pleasant ritual, and helps support the efforts of small, family-owned businesses.

Using seasonal (and ideally, organic and local) produce and ingredients, you can create meals that dazzle the eyes and palate and are incredibly simple to prepare. Eating with the seasons not only helps foster rewarding food traditions, but benefits the environment. Supporting sustainable agriculture reduces our dependence on imported produce, and in effect, the energy required to transport it and the pesticides used to grow it.

It may not be practical to eliminate supermarket shopping

(after all, we do need our paper products and cleaning supplies), but think of ways in which you can "localize" at least some of your food shopping, especially during warmer months. Take full advantage of local foods by joining a CSA farm, shopping at farmer's markets, and picking your own produce. All are superb experiences to share with children, allowing them to see the connection between their foods and their source.

Community Supported Agriculture: What exactly is Community Supported Agriculture? The University of Massachusetts Extension defines it as "a partnership of mutual commitment between a farm and a community of supporters which provides a direct link between the production and consumption of food … CSA members make a commitment to support the farm throughout the season, and assume the costs, risks, and bounty of growing food along with the farmer or grower."
Apart from the obvious benefit of freshly harvested organic produce and special events, CSA members seem to enjoy the ritual of the share pickup, chatting with the growers and fellow members, seeing what produce is new that week, enjoying the scents and colors, then taking it home to the kitchen.

CSAs also foster a sense of community. The one I belong to holds regular potlucks on the farm to connect members, honor the growers and interns, and share food made from the produce. The farm also serves as a springboard for various outreach and charitable activities, and is a catalyst for further social bonds. Ask around about or do a search on CSAs in your area that you might join. They've even started to appear in urban areas.

Farm markets: Hothouse tomatoes, waxed apples, rock-hard peaches, shower-soaked lettuces—welcome to the supermarket produce section. Though this venue for fresh food has improved over the last few years, primped, prepackaged fruits and veggies still serve as reminders that mass-produced produce is bred to look good and last long, rather than taste good. Meant to withstand long rides on trucks and planes, hard and sturdy, not lush and ripe, are the watchwords.

While most supermarket produce sections are serviceable (where would we be without them in winter?), they can't compare with the colorful, fragrant offerings from farm markets and roadside produce stands. Just-picked produce bursts with fragrance and invites touching and comparing.

Here's one instance where impulse buying and letting your senses rule is half the fun. After all, turban squash, fiddlehead ferns, or a peck of habañero peppers may never appear on your shopping list. Farm markets have proliferated in rural as well as urban areas everywhere, so chances are there's one near you. You'll not only enjoy produce that's fresher and riper that anything mass produced, but you will cast a vote for small farms and sustainable agriculture with each dollar you spend.

Farm market excursions are wonderful outings to take with children, who enjoy meeting and talking to the people who produce their food. Visiting a local farmer's market (or taking a field trip to go from one farm stand to another) once a week can easily become a favorite summer and fall tradition. Once you find your favorite stands and get to know the farmers, you'll surely grow to regard these weekly excursions as a favorite food-gathering ritual.

Pick-your-own outings: When my kids were young, they loved to pick berries. Filling wooden baskets with sugary strawberries and blackberries, they gobbled up the small ones like candy; larger berries were used to make toppings for yogurt or ice cream. After a day or two, if there were any left, they'd go into freshly baked muffins or cobbler.

If you live in an urban or suburban area, an annual pick-your-own outing might take some doing, but is well worth the effort. Picking produce is meditative and calming, and the scents of vine-fresh fruits can be intoxicating. From late May through July, look for opportunities to pick berries. If you live within driving distance of apple orchards, an annual apple-picking expedition is a delight. The northwestern U.S. and New Zealand are among the few climates in which it is practical to grow entirely organic apples. So at least, choose an orchard designated as low spray.

Some small farms offer pick-your-own tomatoes in late summer, great for making fresh sauces; you might find venues to pick your own cucumbers, zucchini, green beans, and other veggies to savor immediately or preserve. In October, fall harvest festivals at small farms offer pumpkin picking, a great favorite among small children.

- Deborah recalled a memorable apple-picking outing taken with her family and two others. On a hilltop overlooking the orchard, they segued into a spontaneous picnic, and literally enjoyed the fruits of their labor. Juicy, just-picked apples were washed at outdoor taps and accompanied by pumpkin bread, and cider, purchased from the orchard's market. It was a delicious afternoon, in every sense. Having made apple and pear picking a yearly ritual, Deborah stores

45

the fruit in a large wicker basket on her kitchen floor. Most are eaten out of hand, some made into applesauce, apple or pear cake, and miniature tarts.

- Wendy and her husband began an annual apple-picking ritual when their first son was a Snugli-wrapped infant. Twelve years and three additional children later, a year has not gone by with at least one, and usually more, fruit-picking outings. The family most often frequented a nearby apple farm, spending an entire day, complete with picnic and gorgeous views of a river valley. Now that the family is concerned with the pesticide issue, they prefer to visit farms where they can pick organic berries. What's most appealing, she says, is reaping and gathering food directly from its source—a process we don't get to experience at the supermarket. Wendy has often extended the pleasure of berry-picking outings by making and canning jam—one big batch per fruit picking, ensuring her family the enjoyment of delicious jam all winter long.

Resources

The Greenmarket Cookbook: Recipes, Tips, and Lore from the World Famous Urban Farmers' Market by Joel Patraker, Joan Schwartz gathers recipes and tips from one of the oldest and largest American farm markets.

Preserving Summer's Bounty: A Quick and Easy Guide to Freezing, Canning, Preserving, and Drying What You Grow by Susan McClure is a good guide for those who wish to extend the summer food-gathering season.

. . . .

Part Two

A Miscellany of Family Rituals

*"The family is changing, not disappearing.
We have to broaden our understanding of it, look for
the new metaphors."*

— Mary Catherine Bateson

· ·

Family Reading Rituals

Those of us who were called "bookworms" as girls acquire the more distinctive title of "bibliophile" when we grow up. How can anyone complain of being bored when libraries and bookstores beckon with thousands of unread books? I could live a parallel existence devoted entirely to reading, and I know many others who feel the same!

Still, I frequently hear busy parents bemoan a lack of time, patience, or both, to read for pleasure. Others wonder how to inspire their children to develop a greater love for books. No matter how "educational" certain TV or computer programs are, none are more nourishing than reading. On the contrary, with all that visual stimulus right in your face, the imagination has little chance to take flight, let alone soar.

Reading is surely a wonderful way to spend time alone. But if that kind of time eludes you, establishing rituals of connectedness around books helps ensure that time is carved out for literary pleasures. Reading rituals involving family and friends can be just what's needed to give books their due on an regular basis. These can be as simple as designating a special family reading time, or as sophisticated as forming a book group with a distinct focus.

If I wanted to search for the truth, I could find it in story.
Story can take us far, far beyond fact.

— Madeleine L'Engle

A miscellany of reading rituals

Family reading evenings: Maggie, the mother of three school-age children, has created a cozy family reading ritual. Two evenings a week, the TV, computers, and all other electronic devices are turned off, and everyone convenes in the den for an hour or so of silent reading.

Books and baked goods: An avid baker, Maggie nearly always has wholesome goodies on hand for reading nights. In winter, hot cocoa and a warming fire add a final flourish. A family reading night doesn't necessarily need such distinctive touches, though; it can be as basic as everyone piling into the biggest bed in the house to read silently, or aloud to one another. When older kids and teens have reading to do for school, designated family reading time can make assignments seem less of a chore.

Reading at the table: Most of the time, family dinners should be a time for communication and sharing, but some families designate one evening a week when bringing a book to the table is not only allowed, but encouraged. A simple "nursery food" meal makes this a most comforting pairing of activities. Would you like a bowl of tomato soup and a grilled cheese sandwich with that chapter book?

It's also worth considering reading aloud to your children while they snack or during weekend lunches, rather than parking them in front of the television. Meg Cox, author of *The Heart of a Family*, fondly recalls her favorite mealtime ritual: Living close enough to walk home for lunch during her elementary school years, she remembers her mother reading *Treasure Island* or the *Oz* books to her and her siblings while they ate their Velveeta sandwiches on white bread.

Family book groups: Here's an appealing idea. This kind of book group can include both parents and older kids or teens; it can also include extended family members. It's a fantastic way to connect with grandparents. Teens are especially prone to losing common ground once shared with grandparents; a shared interest in books can span the gap.

Some libraries are now promoting the concept of family book groups, as well as hosting them. If you'd like to keep your family book group private, your library might at least be a good resource for reading lists that appeal to a wide range of ages.

Mother-daughter book groups can be fulfilling for preteen and young teenage girls. This is a nifty way to help them get their wings as readers, while providing a constructive way for growing girls and their mothers to stay connected.

Another way to make a family reading group enticing to older kids and teens is to make it a book-and-film club. Find classic books that have been made into films; read the book first, then watch the movie together on video or DVD (served with plenty of popcorn!). A discussion on the differences as well as the merits of book-versus-movie version can be quite spirited and thought provoking. From classic fiction (*Huckleberry Finn*) to timeless fantasy (*The Lion, the Witch, and the Wardrobe*), this kind of book group is sure to appeal to budding bibliophiles.

Reading Aloud

Establishing a read-aloud ritual can be one of the most gratifying ways to enjoy well-spent family time. If raising children leaves you with little energy or patience for personal reading, take comfort in knowing that reading aloud can be as nourishing for the reader as it is for the listener. And literacy experts agree that reading aloud to your children from an early age helps assure their becoming avid readers later on.

Don't limit reading aloud to preschoolers—school-age children and sometimes even teens love being read to. Add whatever embellishments you'd like—a warm beverage, a specific setting, lots of cuddling—to ensure a prominent place in your child's memory for this time-honored ritual.

Revisit heroines you loved as a child: Reading these books to your own children is a thrill, especially when you can introduce them to heroines you loved as a child. Remember *Betsy-Tacy, Nancy Drew,* Jo March and the rest of the *Little Women, Rebecca of Sunnybrook Farm?* Revel in their tales of spunk and courage while sharing them with your daughters. There's no reason not to try them out on boys, too. Few children can resist *Pippi Longstocking, Pollyanna,* or *Anne of Green Gables.*

It's never too late for a classic: Discovering classics that somehow passed you by is a delight, too. If you somehow missed *Peter Pan, Bambi, Alice in Wonderland, The Secret Garden,* and others as you grew up, share them with your children. Not merely great children's books, but great books altogether, the rich language of classics, experienced aloud, stimulates your imagination as much as your children's.

Fairy and folk tales, ethnic myths, fables, and legends: These make wondrous read-alouds, and their universal themes can be experienced on many levels. Start with the folk stories from your own cultural background, then move on to those of cultures that interest your family.

Create a magical setting: Jennifer not only established a regular time, but an imaginative setting for reading aloud to her children when they were young. With a simple kit, she constructed a "magic house" that they could all snuggle into. Swathing the little structure with a gauzy, rainbow-hued fabric, Jennifer remembers their shared reading time giving them a great sense of safety and cocooning. The diaphanous quality of the light entering their snug shelter, coupled with their favorite stories, was an experience that truly transported them.

Reading aloud for partners: The read-aloud ritual isn't just for parents and children. Instead of crashing out in front of another sitcom or the late news, consider setting aside a quiet hour to read aloud with your partner. Kate and her late husband did just that. Their selection of read-alouds was eclectic, ranging from popular nonfiction (*All Creatures Great and Small* by James Herriot) to classic literature (*Les Miserables* by Victor Hugo); *A Wrinkle in Time* by Madeleine L'Engle, and *The Phantom Tollbooth* by Norton Juster, were among their choices in children's literature. They also explored Arthurian legends and arcane biographies.

What's best about a read-aloud ritual among partners, according to Kate, is "hearing a great story interpreted by your beloved's voice."

"When you read silently, only the writer performs.
When you read aloud, the performance
is collaborative."

— Anne Fadiman, *Ex Libris: Confessions of a Common Reader*

Resources

The Read-Aloud Handbook by Jim Trelease is a definitive volume on this subject. Updated every few years, it makes an inspiring case for reading aloud, and supplies a thorough list of the best read-aloud books for several age groups.

The New York Times' Parent's Guide to the Best Books for Children by Eden Ross Lipson is a guide to children's literature from picture books through young adult novels, with special recommendations for books that make good read-alouds.

Once Upon a Heroine: 450 Books for Girls to Love by Alison Cooper-Mullin and Jennifer Marmaduke Coye explores classic and contemporary literature for girls.

Great Books for Girls: More than 600 Recommended Books for Girls Ages 3-14 by Kathleen Odean lists books for different age groups, featuring strong female characters — fiction and nonfiction.

Great Books for Boys: More than 600 Books for Boys Ages 2–14 by Kathleen Odean is a companion book to the one above, with a masculine slant.

The Heroine's Bookshelf: Life Lessons, from Jane Austen to Laura Ingalls Wilder by Erin Blakemore pairs literature's most beloved heroines, including Jo March, Scarlett O'Hara, and Scout Finch, with their creators to impart wisdom for life's challenges. These intertwined pairs will inspire you to reread your old favorites with your daughters.

Sweet Dreams: Bedtime Rituals for a Good Night

Families with toddlers and young children know that having solid bedtime rituals is critical for maintaining sanity. To hear my husband tell it, I went overboard with the nightly routine when my sons were young. He may be right, but the trade-off was that bedtime was never stressful and almost always a lot of fun. Snacks on a tray, favorite picture books, and above all, the absurd stories told in the dark ensured that bedtime would be anticipated rather than dreaded.

Bedtime routines and rituals have seen reams of print and are often nothing more exciting than a bath, a snack, and reading aloud or a story, done in a consistent, orderly, and loving fashion. Though such rituals are well covered in parenting literature, I enjoyed the clever tips and stories that came my way, and couldn't imagine leaving this topic out. I'd also argue that in families with toddlers and preschool children, the bedtime ritual is more important as a daily ritual than dinner at the table.

When kids go to bed happy, with little resistance, sweet dreams are assured. Here are some ideas:

- Kids adore made-up bedtime stories starring themselves. They can be fairly mundane tales of them taking part in their -favorite activities, interacting with family and friends, or being especially good at something. Weaving the events of the day that has just ended into the "story of your day" is a thrill for small children.

  Recapping the day helps bring order to their many new experiences and sensations—the day's events are "tucked in" along with the child. Of course, kids also love being the central character in an adventure or fantasy tale, if you and your parental imagination are so inclined. One father made his daughters princesses, pirates, and presidents in his nightly stories, having them face and overcome extraordinary hurdles. In stories I told my sons, they interacted with characters from books and movies.

- When older children want to go to bed with their own book, some small ritual of connection can be preserved, like a chat accompanied by warm cocoa or a relaxing back rub.

- Many families tell of a favorite bedtime story ritual in which the story always begins the same way, such as "Once there was an elephant and a mouse." Each family member participating adds a sentence, ensuring that the outcome is amazingly different with each telling.

- In some families, stuffed animals play a role in the nightly ritual. Sometimes they "talk" to the children about what went on in their rooms while they were out of the house; in other instances, they are set up to patrol the room while the children sleep, keeping them safe from monsters and unpleasant dreams.

- If you're not much of a storyteller, start a "Bedtime Q&A" tradition, suggests Alicia. "When you tuck in your child, designate some time to ask questions about the day or about life in general. You could make it structured, every night asking what was something they learned, what was something good that happened and something bad . . . and then you should answer too. Or you can ask different questions of each other every night—everything from what sort of tree do you think you'd be to who do you most admire."

- Jennifer and her two children have long enjoyed a tradition of winding down their day by sharing a big platter of nicely arranged fruit served on her king-sized bed. Everyone piles in to eat fruit, chat, and cuddle. Often, even the dog joins in. Jennifer thinks that each day needs to end with lots of cuddling. Having lived in Europe, where more affection is displayed, she feels that Americans need to be more demonstrative.

- Some parents sing special songs to lull their kids to sleep (and others use more boisterous or silly songs to get them up in the morning). Deb has always included singing in her daughter's bedtime ritual. A particular song was sung, until such time as another would take its place. Memorable ones included *Sweet Baby James* (James Taylor), *The Man in the Moon* (Mary Chapin Carpenter), and *The Circle Game* (Joni Mitchell).

- Before bedtime, do gentle stretches with your children to release tension—yours and theirs. Yoga postures such as Child's Pose are also relaxing, as is lying face up, palms up, visualizing each part of the body, then releasing any tension held there. A number of books on yoga for children are available; see which suits your needs.

- Lisa recalled a number of relaxation rituals that her children enjoyed when they were very young. During winter months, she tucked a hot water bottle in with each child to keep them toasty while they heard their bedtime stories. They also play a game called "listen to the silence," during which they listen for a couple of minutes, then relate what they've heard—a passing car, breathing, the rumbling of a tummy.

- Visualization can be a creative way to get your children from an active, alert state to a restful one. In a darkened room, talk them through a relaxing scenario—for example, describe to your child in a soothing voice how he or she is walking on a beach, listening to the waves break, watching the wispy clouds in the sky. Once in a while, a dolphin leaps out of the water, and a beautiful shell is picked up and admired.

"I hated to see bedtime rituals end with my children. I remember when my son was about 13, and said two nights in a row that he didn't want to talk that night. The second time I asked, 'Shall we leave it that you ask me if you want to talk?' I knew it was over. I found my wife downstairs, and cried."

— William J. Doherty, *The Intentional Family*

. . . . .

Family Meeting

"When we were children, families shared mealtimes, leisurely summer evenings on the patio, weekly worship services, and long car trips to grandmother's house," write Elaine Hightower and Betsy Riley in *Our Family Meeting Book.* "Families didn't need meetings because they hashed out mutual concerns around the dinner table. But with both parents working and children participating in more structured activities than ever before, hectic schedules are squeezing out the household rituals which bonded past generations."

Apparently, today's families do need meetings. It's a growing trend—structuring a day, time, and agenda to convene as a family and explore issues, arrange schedules, take care of nuts-and-bolts items, and air both appreciation and gripes.

For ten years, Jane, her husband, and son held a family meeting every Sunday. The ritual was sweetened by preceding it with a special brunch. Family meetings followed a pattern that Jane and Steve gleaned from a communication retreat, which created a productive structure to follow. The three of them also coordinated their plans for the week, noting special events or changes in schedule. Jane says that their Sunday brunch-and-meeting ritual was something to count on and an ideal way launch their busy weeks.

When their teenage son began sleeping until all hours of the day on Sunday, Jane sensed that this ritual was about to shift. Once their son left for college, the weekly meetings ended by necessity. She misses it, of course, but still enjoys a leisurely Sunday brunch with her husband.

Here's a sample schedule to follow for family meetings:

- Start out with positives and good news.

- Go on to "business"—schedules and activities for the up-coming week, as well as things that need to be done (talk to Tommy's teacher about the math test) or bought (Tara needs sneakers).

- Proceed with gripes and debates, but don't allow them to deteriorate into petty arguments.

- Explore a topic of mutual interest to everyone, such as: What can we do to help Grandma more often? How can we earn extra money to buy a trampoline? Or weightier issues, like: What companies should we boycott because they are polluters? What kind of donation should we make to the food bank for Thanksgiving?

- End the meeting by making positive resolutions.

"If we as parents want to pass on our values and raise strong, confident children, we have to be more deliberate about our parenting. Holding family meetings is one of the quickest, easiest ways to improve communication and build character within our families."

— Elaine Hightower and Betsy Riley,
Our Family Meeting Book

Resource

Our Family Meeting Book: Fun and Easy Ways to Manage Time, Build Communication, and Share Responsibility Week by Week by Elaine Hightower and Betsy Riley is a workbook filled with inspiration and ideas for those who want lots of great ideas for kick-starting a family meeting ritual. Fifty-two sample weekly themes (such as "What Does Our Family Stand For?" —exploring values, and "Taking your chances"—about risk) are suggested to set the tone or spark discussion. The book shows how to use the family meeting to deal with conflict resolution, create family traditions, set goals and plan activities, celebrate accomplishments, and much more.

Volunteering as a Family

Many busy families wish they had more time to volunteer for causes they believe in or to give something back to their communities. But lest you think it's an impossible dream, a recent survey by Youth Service America reports that teen volunteerism is at an all-time high, indicating a strong level of idealism.

Community service is often a high school requirement, and in many cases, once teens get a taste of it, they want to do more. That desire can be instilled in children, even from a very early age. To make volunteering a part of your family life, create a tradition by making it a regularly scheduled event, whether once a month or once a year. The key is finding a cause that stirs everyone's passions.

Lee's family chose a food pantry called the Cooperative Feeding Program to focus on. For many years, they volunteered in tandem, stocking shelves and serving food. They also take part in an annual food drive called the Postal Carrier's Food Drive, taking place each Mother's Day weekend. They help collect and pack tons of food that people have put in their mailboxes. The boxes are then delivered to the Cooperative Feeding Program. By focusing on one charity, and staying involved over a number of years, this family built a tradition of which they can be proud.

If your family can choose only one big event each year to participate in, consider a walkathon. In many communities, charitable organizations sponsor walkathons to raise money for various causes, particularly to raise research money for disease prevention. Another worthy annual event to consider is participating in the cleanup of a public place, especially ecologically sensitive areas. Inquire with environmental organizations in your area.

Jenny Friedman was a freelance writer when her daughters were young. At the time, she felt a great urge to give something back to her community, but wanted to do something that would allow her to have her daughters (then just three years old and six months old) with her. She and a friend, who also had a three-year-old, came up with the idea of delivering meals together to the homebound, through the Meals on Wheels agency.

The two friends would pile the kids into one car, pick up the meals, and make about ten deliveries, twice a month. They took turns staying in the car with the baby while the other would take the two three-year-olds to the doors. The little girls would hand the meals to the elderly or homebound, who would invariably be delighted to see them. Even at so tender an age, the girls gained a lot from the experience—they especially loved all the attention, which made them feel quite important!

Jenny and her friend realized that this volunteer work was actually better with their children than it would have been without them; the extra helping of happiness that came with the plate of food made a big difference. This also got her thinking further about the benefits of doing community service as a family. As her family grew (a son came along later), so did her interest in the subject, which culminated in her writing the ultimate guide creating family volunteering traditions — *The Busy Family's Guide to Volunteering.*

"Each time we volunteer," she writes, "we have an opportunity to teach our children that every human being has worth, that we are stewards of this planet, that the world is a better place when we care for others and they care for us." Admitting that finding the time to volunteer can be an obstacle for any family, she reminds us that "lessons can be taught, people's lives changed, and small miracles wrought in only minutes or hours."

Jenny Friedman's guide breaks down the resistance and guilt barriers by showing how fun and gratifying volunteering can be when done as a family. A plethora of opportunities in many areas of interest are explored, with specifics on how to get started. There are the more predictable yet worthy venues of volunteerism, including working with the elderly, hungry, and homeless, and supporting the causes of environment and animal welfare.

She also suggests avenues that may not immediately come to mind, such as arts, literacy, peace, and social justice organizations. One of my children participated with a high school team in a local spelling bee to raise money and awareness for Literacy Volunteers of America. It was so much fun that she participated again next year, and I, too, have been inspired to participate in future bees with a friend. An annual tradition is born!

The approach of the winter holiday season and its attendant good will can provide a good catalyst for getting into charitable mode. There are so many traditions of giving that you can initiate at this time of year—serving food in a soup kitchen on

Thanksgiving, delivering holiday food baskets to the elderly and homebound, participating in toy drives, adopting a low-income family and helping with their holiday needs.

The Points of Light Foundation sponsors two national events that can serve as springboards for starting family volunteering traditions. The first is Make a Difference Day, falling on the fourth Saturday each October. Visit www.makeadifferenceday.com to find and register projects and get ideas based on what others have done.

Next, National Family Volunteer Day takes place on the Saturday before each Thanksgiving. This event is "designed to showcase the benefits of families working together, to introduce community service, and encourage those who haven't yet made the commitment to volunteer as a family." It's an ideal way to kick-start a ritual of volunteerism for your family. Visit www.pointsoflight.org to find out more.

Show your kids that it's easy to make a difference. Cement volunteerism into your family's values by making it a tradition, whether one day a year, or a half day per month, or an hour a week.

"Reclaim your influence and your vital role in a world you can change. You'll discover that the difference a day makes, while significant for the recipients, is greatest for the giver."

— Karen M. Jones, *The Difference a Day Makes*

Resources

The Busy Family's Guide to Volunteering: Do Good, Have Fun, Make a Difference as a Family by Jenny Lynne Friedman is an excellent resource, extensively described in this section.

A Kid's Guide to Service Projects: Over 500 Service Ideas for Young People Who Want to Make a Difference by Barbara Lewis is another great book with ideas in dozens of areas of volunteerism.

Catch the Spirit: Teen Volunteers Tell How They Made a Difference by Susan K. Perry, is meant to inspire older kids and teens.

The Giving Box: Create a Tradition of Giving with Your Children by Fred Rogers is a gently inspiring book by the late television personality.

The Difference a Day Makes: 365 Ways to Change Your World in Just 24 Hours by Karen M. Jones provides a simple way to make a difference each day in areas including ecology, peace, health, child welfare, and much more.

. . . . .

Family Rituals in Brief

Family Traditions Calendar: What better way to preserve all the special dates and occasions you want to mark than by designating a calendar specifically for family traditions? It need not be anything more elaborate than a medium-sized month-by-month wall calendar; if you use one of these, you can hang it up where it will be visible by all, but you will need to transfer in the dates anew each year.

An alternative to this is to use a "Book of Days" type datebook that remains valid from one year to the next. With either format, use the calendar to mark family birthdays, anniversaries, and unique celebrations and activities (such as "Picasso's birthday," "The day we adopted Mittens," or "Our annual camping trip").

Don't use the family traditions calendar to mark down dental appointments, soccer practice, one-time events — save those for your appointment calendar. If you use a book of days as your family traditions calendar, you can also use some of the spaces to record favorite memories and events that occurred on specific dates.

Friday night at the home movies: A surprising number of families I spoke with enjoy ordering pizza and watching movies at home on Friday evenings. While on a yearlong sabbatical in Cambridge, England, Carlie and her family continued their Friday evening pizza tradition (though she had to make the pizza herself to approximate the American version).

They found this ritual especially relaxing after a week of school and work in a place where the language was similar, but the culture very different. Other families reported enjoying their pizza picnic-style at home, on an old blanket in the den, while watching their Friday night movie.

On the surface, pizza and movies might hardly qualify as a ritual, though it's amazing how many families who practice it deliberately avoid making other plans on Friday evenings! It's a simple, inexpensive way to recharge the family's collective batteries, and especially relaxing for home cooks who rarely rely on take-out meals.

"Firsts and lasts": Simple rituals make milestones memorable and significant. Ritual expert Barbara Biziou devised a "last day" ritual with her son to mark the last day of school or camp, the final soccer game of the season, and such. For these occasions, she and her son would enjoy a quiet, candlelit pizza dinner, to reflect on what he would miss about the experience.

Creating your own simple ceremonies for acknowledging firsts and lasts helps children recognize the small but significant passages that go into growing up. I think it's wonderful to make a big deal of graduating elementary school and middle school, not just high school and college. We didn't do so for our kids, and I regret it, so we'll really need to do something big when they finish high school! Think of how you can mark the first tooth lost, first period, first report card, last day of summer vacation, last game of the season, receiving a driver's license, and other milestones, with fun, simple ceremonies.

Family game night: Just a generation ago, most family members were actually home, spending time together in the evening. Who needed a ritual for this? For many of today's families, though, spending an evening at home, playing together, can seem like a revolutionary idea. Some families enjoy having a focus for this together time and have designated an evening per week, especially in colder months, for playing classic board games.

A variation on this is working on a jigsaw puzzle together while listening to music or radio programs. An ideal game night takes place after dinner and cleanup; Friday night works well, since homework is not an issue and bedtime is more flexible; otherwise, early Sunday evening works well, and is a nice way to end the weekend.

Spending time together playing classic board games may not seem like such a big deal. But this activity is a delightful memory-maker and offers opportunities, especially for younger children to learn fair play, exercise patience, follow rules, and win and lose gracefully. Board games like the ones you grew up with are not only fun, but build skills and sharpen mental agility.

Building neighborhood connections: Neighborhoods provide a convenient venue for traditions of friendship and connection, and yet they are sadly underused—promises of "Someday, we'll have a block party" usually mean it probably won't happen. In truth, organizing a block party can be as easy as choosing a date and a central location on the street, and putting a flyer in mailboxes designating a date and location, and asking everyone to bring snacks and games to share. Potlucks, neighborhood yard sales, holidays, games, and sports can all provide focal points for neighborhood traditions. Consider:

- An annual yard sale or "swap meet," followed by a block party. Any unsold or unswapped merchandise can then be gathered and donated to a local charity.

- A number of families, couples, or individuals meeting for a monthly potluck and game night. In Sandy's neighborhood, four couples rotate among one another's homes for an evening of dessert and Scrabble.

- In Anne's neighborhood, one or more of any number of neighborhood women set out for an after-dinner walk. As they pass by the houses of others in this network, more and more women join up as they spot the group passing by their houses. It's a nice way to connect on warm, pleasant evenings, and has turned neighbors into friends.

  An outdoor "farewell to summer" gathering at a local pool or park, with a potluck barbecue and conversation for the adults; games and swimming for kids.

- A neighborhood open house to view winter holiday season decor and share hot chocolate and cookies (or wine and appetizers) is a splendid way to kick off the holiday season before everyone gets busy with family gatherings and travel.

Sporting traditions: In an age when the many families need more physical activity and just plain fresh air, it can be useful as well as fun to build simple rituals and traditions around sports and athletic pursuits. There are numerous forms that this can take, from a weekly family hike, to a seasonal event (a canoe or bicycle trip each spring), to a single big annual event (like the neighborhood softball game and barbecue celebrated on the last day of school by Mary and her neighbors).

A shared athletic activity can become a rite of passage event;

in a couple of families I know of, Dad treats each child on his or her first ski trip, one-on-one, once they reach a certain age.

Some families complain that team sports take over their lives while their kids are involved in them. While these can undoubtedly be a burden, others have been fortunate enough to be able to add a few little rituals that make school sports feel more inclusive and less obtrusive. Susie's older son was involved in competitive running during high school, and the parents as well as their kids were totally immersed in the experience, making the season an enjoyable community activity. The parents volunteered to do timing at the finish line or work the concession stand.

Other family sporting traditions can include a weekly bowling outing; regular skating or cross-country ski outings in the winter; a yearly camping trip to a favorite destination that includes hiking, climbing, and/or swimming. When spring rolls around, my husband and younger son know it's time to hoist the canoe onto the top of the car and explore local lakes and swamps. What sporting traditions can you incorporate into your family's repertoire?

Share your passions with your children: Whether you have one child or several, a hectic schedule can leave you feeling that any or all are getting short shrift. Of course, there is nothing wrong with simply scheduling a regular date with each child to go out to eat, or go out for ice cream and a walk—anything that allows for interaction.

An even more creative way to use together time is to share those things with your child that you thought you'd have to shelve until they were grown. If you love music, nature, fine cuisine, making pottery, or outdoor adventure, share these passions with your children by creating rituals, as they become age-appropriate. It makes children feel grown-up and very much included to participate in those activities for which you have obvious enthusiasm. One mother of two daughters told me of a regular activity the three shared as the girls grew up that she called "sharing skills." Through the years, they shared "massages, painting, cooking, music, jewelry making, weaving, and a lot more," as she recalled. Not surprisingly, both young women are now in art school.

Part Three

Celebrating, Commemorating, and Preserving Memories

"Share our similarities, celebrate our differences."

—M. Scott Peck

They say it's your birthday

After reaching a certain age, my husband and I grew weary of celebrating our birthdays. Even the birthday celebrations for our young children were taking on the forced gaiety of New Year's Eve parties. Planning parties for the kids became a grind, consisting of:

a) choosing a place to gather a bunch of school friends to do an activity for two hours,

b) receiving unneeded gifts,

c) and breathing a sigh of relief when the kids were picked up by their parents.

When I mentioned these "birthday blues" to a friend, she said that birthdays, in her mind, are a way to celebrate the person and to show appreciation for them. Out of 365 days of the year, one of them should have your name on it. That helped cast a new light on the subject for me. At its best, a birthday can be dedicated to appreciating and honoring the celebrant. Like small, daily rituals of connection, this special celebration need not include fancy or creative elements, but rather those that are meaningful to the birthday boy or girl, whether of the young or grown-up variety.

A meal designed around the birthday person's favorite dishes, or an outing to the restaurant of their choice; a few words of appreciation spoken around the table after the candles are blown out; gifts that are truly useful and have meaning; a day trip to a much-loved place; a "birthday book" detailing accomplishments of the past year—these and other personal touches can add up to a truly personal and happy birthday. Here are some ideas to make this common ritual more meaningful.

Birthday letters: Instead of buying store-bought cards, writing birthday letters is a ritual shared by Shannon, a single mother, and her three children, ages fourteen, eleven, and nine. Each family member receives a letter from the others on their birthday, ranging from single-page notes to multipage extravaganzas filled with stickers, drawings, and memorabilia.

"I think these letters help the kids to think about what they love about their siblings," said Shannon. "They write such amazing letters to each other! In my letters to them, I focus on their accomplishments of the last year, how they've grown, and the steps they've taken toward independence. Getting the letters they write to me is the best part of my birthday. They prove that I'm definitely not taken for granted. If I had to make a quick escape from my house and could only grab one thing, it would be the box of birthday letters from my children."

Andrea described in equally affection terms the birthday letter her mother gave her from the time she was five until she graduated high school. She always included a few photos as well. At first, she found the birthday letters were thrilling, but by the time she reached high school, they seemed rather corny and embarrassing. Still, she kept them through the years, and now, long after her mother was gone and her own kids grown, she considers this collection of letters priceless.

"I shared my mother's birthday letters with my kids when they were in their early teens, and let me tell you, it was an eye-opener for them!" said Andrea. "They were able to imagine my childhood more vividly and see all the common threads between themselves and me. I wrote birthday letters to my children

. . . .
: to time, though far less consistently and thoroughly
mother did for me. This is something I honestly regret,
I hope to make up for with my first granddaughter,
who .. s recently born. I look forward to creating birthday letters for her as well as any future grandchildren."

Birthday book: With a little more effort than goes into birthday letters, you can create a yearly "birthday book" for your children. This need not be an entire, extravagant scrapbook; you can keep it simple and take four pieces of sturdy 9-by-12-inch colored paper, folded in half to make an instant sixteen-page booklet.

This idea comes from Dawnesha, who makes a birthday book each year for her daughters. She pastes in a few recent photos; school information; names and possible photos of current friends; ticket stubs from special events attended; awards; and other memorabilia; listings of likes, dislikes, hobbies, and passions. Not only is the birthday book fun to make as an annual ritual, she says, but each year, all the previous birthday books are brought out, in itself an enjoyable ritual of reminiscence.

Birthday basket: Placing a "birthday basket" on the kitchen table (or other central location) a week or so before a family member's birthday is a simple and fun ritual. In it, the other family members can place cards, informal notes and thoughts, tiny gifts and "I.O.U." coupons that hold promises of special one-on-one times for a movie and dinner night out (promised either by the child or the parent), reprieves from chores, or other favors to be granted. On the day of that person's birthday, wake them up to a birthday breakfast and have them open all the small surprises in their birthday basket.

Simple gifting: *The Simple Living Guide* author Janet Luhrs lists several wonderful, low-impact ideas for birthday gift giving. Asking the guests to bring used toys, books, and sports equipment in good condition to trade can result in a fun "swap meet."

Another great idea is to put together a coupon book for the birthday child. Before the party date, ask all the guests to contribute one I.O.U.-type gift. Some examples Luhrs gives are: a sleepover; an afternoon at a favorite bookstore, entitling the birthday child to choose one book to buy; dinner at a friend's house; a weekend date for swimming, horseback riding, etc. Friends as well as family members can contribute to the coupon book. Finally, Luhrs suggests having all the guests bring one of their own toys or books, gift wrapped. The party hosts have a raffle and everyone gets one gift.

Recounting their arrival: For younger children, it's a thrill to hear the story of their arrival into the world as part of the birthday celebration. Build drama into the tale by including details of the anticipation of this wondrous event! Finally, embellish the story by pulling out the first photo taken of them, the certificate that bears their tiny footprint, their tiny nursery cap, and any other memorabilia you have to share.

"Birthday dates" with the kids: When David was about eight years old, he decided to take his mother out for a birthday breakfast. With plenty of choices at hand, he proudly chose a truck stop diner, where every meal cost $1.39. "Mom," he said as he waved his hand expansively toward the menu, "order anything you want."

And so began a "birthday breakfast" tradition that lasted for some years. David's still prefers a gift of one-on-one time from her now-grown sons for her birthday. For some years now, she and each son try to have a special date around the time of her birthday. It's usually something simple, like a special breakfast, dinner and/or a movie, but it's far more meaningful to her than receiving a purchased gift.

Kids can be unsure what to buy for their parents' birthday (and often have limited means), so expressing a preference for shared time can be a blessing for the giver and receiver alike. Having kids make a standing date to spend with grandparents on their birthdays is an equally thoughtful and gratifying ritual.

Seasonal connections: Link your own cyclic rhythms and the earth's. Your birthday is a perfect occasion to celebrate in a meaningful way that reflects the season of your birth. I have a favorite ritual for my mid-spring birthday, when our region is beginning to blossom, and the days grow longer and warmer.

My family and I go to a beautiful land preserve that's both serene and stunningly beautiful. We hike to an observation tower, from which we can see five states on a clear day; we canoe or paddle boat on a small jewel of a lake; we scramble through rock formations; and we stop for a picnic at Lily Pond, which teems with new life—tadpoles, baby turtles, and fish. This yearly ritual helps me begin another chapter of my life with a renewed sense of hope and the promise of adventure.

The big giveaway: Prior to birthdays (as well as major holidays), it's good to convey to children the importance of making space and sharing what is outgrown or no longer needed. Both of Marina's children's birthdays are in mid-November, so she tries to make this an annual ritual that's fun, and promotes a sense of generosity. Three or more boxes are prepared, marked

"Women's shelter," "For friends," and "Thrift shop." She lets the girls give items to friends, and when they were old enough, she began taking them to personally deliver clothes, toys, and books to a local shelter so they could see their giving in action.

"New Privilege, New Responsibility": Gertrud Mueller Nelson, author of *To Dance with God: Family Ritual and Celebration*, writes of a ritual that is also a mini rite of passage for each year. On their birthdays, she gave her children two envelopes: One was marked "New Privilege" and the other, "New Responsibility." A child turning six might be given the privilege of staying up an extra half hour at night, and the responsibility of feeding the dog its dinner. This ritual, writes the author, "gave them a sense of importance and made them feel grown up."

Document the day: Many of us get lax about photographing and videotaping our kids on a regular basis; make sure to use the occasion of their birthday to do so. You can use a mini photo album for each year, date it, and store in a photo box. Date and store each videotape in a specially designated "birthday box." The fun part is revisiting these memories in subsequent years, and this, in fact, can become part of each year's birthday ritual.

Birthday customs, ancient and modern

Your children might enjoy knowing the meaning behind some of our deeply ingrained birthday customs, such as why we have birthday cake and blow out candles. Similarly, learning about birthday customs from around the world, and perhaps incorporating some of them into our own celebrations, can add an offbeat spark that keep festivities from becoming rote.

- It's commonly accepted that many modern birthday customs originated in 19th-century Germany, particularly the traditions of parties, cakes, and blowing out candles. Candle making was quite an art in Germany, and this is believed to be the place where setting small candles on cakes got started. Blowing out all candles at once was thought to bring good luck, which later came to symbolize having one's wishes granted.

- The cake-and-candles custom may have had even earlier roots: Legend has it that the ancient Greeks once took round cakes, to represent the full moon, to the temple of the goddess of the moon, Artemis. Candles were put on the cake to represent the glowing moon.

- It's not uncommon to find American children taking aim at piñatas at birthday parties. This custom originated in Mexico, of course. In this three-hundred-year-old tradition, piñatas are filled with candies and treats shaped as animals or stars.

- In Japan, all birthdays were once celebrated on January 1, no matter when the person's actual birth date. It was a national day of birthdays! Today, most Japanese people celebrate their birthday on the true date on which they were born. One modern custom is for the birthday person to wear an entirely new set of clothes for the occasion.

- In China, a common birthday custom is to invite relatives and friends to lunch and serve long noodles to symbolize a long life for the child.

- In the British Isles, one charming tradition was serving "fortune telling cake" to the birthday person. Small symbolic objects were baked into the birthday cake. Finding a coin in one's piece of cake, for example, foretold future riches.

- In India, it was customary for the birthday child to wear particularly brightly colored clothing and to distribute chocolates to classmates.

- In Israel, the birthday child sits in a chair. His or her family and friends raise and lower the child in the chair, the number of "raises" corresponding with the child's age, plus one more for good luck.

- Finally, what can you do for that rare child who doesn't care for cake? Do what has long been done in Russia and make a birthday pie, with a greeting carved into the crust.

Resources

Happy Birthday, Everywhere! by Arlene Erlbach is filled with ideas on customs, games, and recipes for children's birthdays from around the globe.

The Ultimate Birthday Party Book: 50 Complete and Creative Themes to Make Your Kid's Special Day Fantastic! by Susan Baltrus offers fun thematic ideas for out-of-the-ordinary birthdays.

The Penny Whistle Birthday Party Book by Meredith Brokaw and Annie Gilbar explores a myriad of ideas for fun birthday parties at home.

Creating Unique Family Celebrations

The spirit craves celebration through occasions set apart from the ordinary. If the celebratory rites you grew up with no longer resonate, or if you simply wish to make them more surprising and less rote, gather with your family, turn on the creative juices, and explore how you can create celebrations that are meaningful to all of you.

This section will concern itself more with smaller and unique celebrations rather than the traditional holidays. However, whether or not you celebrate traditional holidays (and I'm in no way suggesting that you abandon your traditions), why not think of marking special occasions, large or small, personal or universal, in ways that are unique to your family? You might also consider giving existing traditions a fresh spin that suits the needs and beliefs of your family. For example:

- Amanda's favorite holiday had always been Thanksgiving, but after her divorce and parents' deaths, the day felt more depressing than festive. With two preteens at home, she still wanted to so something meaningful as well as fun. Though the kids fought it tooth and nail at first, Amanda decided that the three of them should volunteer at a local soup kitchen.

  They helped serve the Thanksgiving meal around noon, leaving much of the rest of the day to do something for themselves. Amanda also organized a potluck dinner for others whose families lived far away or who, for various reasons, had no plans for Thanksgiving. Years later, Amanda still enjoys this rewarding recasting of her favorite holiday. Her son and daughter are now in college, and occasionally spend Thanksgiving break with their father or a friend, but their mom's Thanksgiving tradition—especially the volunteering—rates highest with them.

- Cynthia and her husband each have several siblings, so Christmas gift-buying had become daunting as their families grew. Though they still buy gifts for all the nieces and nephews, the adults decided that they would make small donations in one another's name to that person's favorite charity.

- Terry's family no longer ascribes to the religious aspects of Passover, but didn't want to "do nothing," as she puts it, on this important Jewish holiday. "I still wanted us to feel connected to Jews around the world." Her family and guests still have a festive meal on the first night of Passover. However, instead of the traditional Seder, they serve foods that celebrate spring, and read passages of their choosing on the meaning of freedom, a central theme of this holiday.

- Kwanzaa is a prime example of how holiday hoopla can be transformed into meaningful ceremony. A modern holiday with ancient roots, it was first celebrated in 1966 after being developed by Dr. Maulana Karenga (then chair of the department of Black Studies at California State University, Long Beach), to underscore the need to preserve African American culture.
  Though celebrated from December 26 through January 1, Kwanzaa is not religious and avoids commercial trappings, instead focusing on family, community, and culture. Dr. Karenga drew its principles, and its name, from the

81

first harvest celebrations of Africa. Celebrating the cultures of a number of African communities, it is now practiced by millions of Africans of all faiths and languages throughout the world! One man's creation of a celebration now so beloved by families around the globe can surely inspire individual families to design festive rituals with special meaning for themselves.

It is for each family to decide which holidays traditional to their own cultural background to celebrate, to what extent, and with what unique elements. Holidays and celebrations can be the most daunting for those in single-parent families and mixed-tradition partnerships, but these circumstances can also allow for the most creativity. Consult the resources at the end of this section for many excellent ideas.

> *"Our homes need revelry as much as we do. Few things enliven a residence as thoroughly as giving it a reputation for celebration. Every holiday marked there, every congratulatory dinner, every open house honoring visitors from far away—these add up to make your house or apartment a place that radiates warmth, hospitality, and memories by the roomful."*
>
> — Victoria Moran, *Shelter for the Spirit*

Borrow from other cultures: If there's a culture that fascinates you or any members of your family, borrow from it to create festive celebrations. New Year celebrations, harvest festivals, seasonal and celestial rites, and other nondenominational holidays can give your family a fresh, exciting perspective and teach children to appreciate cultures other than their own.

Even a superficial nod to the celebratory rituals of global cultures helps foster tolerance in a world growing ever smaller. Acknowledging Cinco de Mayo (Mexican Independence Day), Diwali (the Hindu Festival of Lights), or the Chinese New Year, is cultural education disguised as fun. There are plenty of books on these subjects geared to kids, and lots of information on the internet.

Chinese culture has fascinated my son ever since he studied it in second grade. Thanks to him, we've been celebrating the Chinese New Year for some years. At the start of this two-week festival, he decorates our kitchen with his dragon collection and creates a centerpiece with dragons, candles, oranges, and the customary coin-filled red envelopes. On the first night, we enjoy a homemade Chinese meal. One year, we attended a festive celebration hosted by the local Chinese community, another, we attended a performance of the Beijing acrobats.

Each year, we add a little something to the celebration; it has become a tradition that adds shimmer to the dismal days of February.

Similarly, multiethnic rituals can be woven into standard holidays to make them a richer experience. Take the New Year celebration, for instance. Many of us find this an occasion of forced gaiety, devoid of either meaning or real fun. Instead of watching the televised ball drop on Times Square, consider some traditions from around the world to add spark to family New Year celebrations. Here are a few customs from cultures that celebrate the New Year on January first, so we can catch their spirit:

- In Finland, the New Year is really played up, as it comes at the darkest time of year, when daylight is scarce indeed. A light meal, sauna, and fireworks are customary. The Finns also play games to foretell the future on New Year's Eve. This traditionally has taken the form of a melted piece of tin in a container of water—something a bit arcane for us non-Finns. Try a ready-made form of divination, such as tarot cards or the *I Ching*. Explore these and other divination tools at a New Age shop as part of the fun.

- Numerous traditions are associated with the Japanese New Year. Friends and family forgive one another for any disagreements, so that everyone can start the new year fresh. On December 31, bells or gongs are rung 108 times to dispel 108 troubles, followed by gales of laughter, in the belief that laughing drives away troubles and bad spirits. With the spirit of forgiveness, and with all troubles driven away, a day of celebration follows.

- Eat twelve grapes at the stroke of midnight, as is the custom in Spain. Each grape, representing one month of the year, is eaten for every stroke of the clock. This custom is believed to bring good luck in the new year.

Celebrate your heroes and heroines: Celebrating the birthdays of great thinkers, authors, and leaders is a fantastic way to teach kids about cultural icons. When Victoria's daughter was young, they enjoyed celebrating Mozart's birihday. If you admire Gandhi, commemorating his birthday is an opportunity to honor his wisdom and compassion. Is there an author, poet, or musician that your family particularly admires?

For youngsters, celebrating the birthdays of classic authors can be a rollicking good time. Imagine a "Mad Hatter's tea party" for Lewis Carroll, a picnic highlighting honey-flavored goodies for Winnie-the-Pooh creator A.A. Milne, and for Dr. Seuss — well, anything goes.

Celebrate smaller holidays: If you don't wish to create your own celebrations "from scratch," take cues from what is already on the calendar, which offers ample opportunities for small celebrations throughout the year. Explore how you can tailor them to your family's liking.

Groundhog Day, for instance, coming at one of the year's dreariest times, can be an occasion to create traditions for coaxing spring (planting seedlings in pots, bringing in branches of flowering shrubs to force indoors). Or, watch the wonderful movie of the same name accompanied by a meal consisting of your family's favorite cold-weather comfort foods—served on a picnic blanket on the floor. Here's a good example of how just one month offers lots of small occasions to celebrate. Far from being the proverbial "cruelest month," April offers ample opportunities beyond the major holidays of Easter and Passover:

- April is National Poetry Month. Have everyone bring a favorite poem to share at the dinner table once a week, or make it a month to read poetry at bedtime instead of stories.

- April Fool's Day can be celebrated with humor (rather than playing pranks). Read favorite humor books aloud, and watch classic comedies.

- Earth Day falls on April 22, and many communities offer an abundance of activities for families. You can participate in those, or fashion your own earth-friendly tradition, such as cleanup of a favorite park or shore path. Earth Day Network (www.earthday.net) is a site devoted to celebrating Earth Day on April 22 and throughout the year.

- Arbor Day, which usually falls on the last Friday in April, can inspire your family to create a yearly tree-planting ceremony. National Arbor Day Foundation (www.arbor-day.org): For a nominal membership fee, this organization will mail you ten young trees to plant that are just right for your part of the country, with instructions and tips for maintenance.

The turning of the seasons also offers many opportunities for small rites of celebration.

Resources

The Book of New Family Traditions: How to Create Great Rituals for Holidays and Everyday by Meg Cox has lots of ideas for making traditional and smaller holidays more fun, especially for younger children.

New Traditions: Redefining Celebrations for Today's Family by Susan Abel Lieberman is also an excellent book on giving fresh life to customary holidays and traditional celebrations (like anniversaries, Mother's Day, and such). The author doesn't shy away from addressing issues like divorce and unconventional families in this context.

· ·

Kids Around the World Celebrate! The Best Feasts and Festivals from Many Lands by Lynda Jones is a book of lore and recipes for multicultural holidays.

The Official Kwanzaa Web Site (officialkwanzaawebsite.org) was created by its originator, Dr. Maulana Karenga. And most any library system has many, many books on Kwanzaa aimed at young readers, with lore, crafts, activities, and recipes.

> *"When old traditions lose their vitality or cease to serve, we should unravel them and mix old threads with new to weave new family traditions than give us shared experiences and togetherness."*
>
> — Susan Abel-Lieberman, *New Traditions*

Preserving Family Memories

Taking regular pictures and video of your children and family adventures, then organizing them in some chronological fashion is admirable (and more than most parents manage to do!). Keeping physical scrapbooks and boxes of memorabilia is no small feat in this digital age, but pulling them out from time to time to reminisce over is a priceless pleasure.

Though it may often seem daunting, no one regrets the investment of time put into preserving family photos and memorabilia, no matter what shape the endeavor takes. For these purposes, though, let's look at a few ways to turn the process of preserving family memories into fun traditions.

Take a photo at the same time and place each year: Maria and her husband planted a tree to honor the birth of each of their three children, reflecting an ancient custom shared by many cultures. From the time each child could stand, he or she was photographed on their birthday, next to their special tree. The photos serve a poignant reminder of the fleeting nature of childhood, yet at the same time they are anchors, rooting each child in time and place.

From the time they were eight and ten years old, Janice and Becky's father has taken their photo together on a bench in front of their family's lake cottage. The photo has always been taken on or around the Fourth of July. Thirty years later, the sisters feel fortunate that their father is still in good health and willing to take their tandem photo on that same bench any time they happen to visit their parents together during the summer.

Stacie feels that the annual family reunion she hosts each summer wouldn't be complete without a photograph of the entire clan of aunts, uncles, siblings, and cousins. To extend the pleasure of this same-time, same place ritual, you can create a chronological display of the photos somewhere in your home.

Create a time capsule: Here's an easy, engaging activity, ideal for doing during the lull between the winter holidays and New Year's Day, when the old year is winding down (though any time you find more convenient is fine). It takes but a few fun-filled hours, and creates a concrete link to your family's history as well as the culture at large, for many years to come. Choose a sturdy plastic storage container, the size of a shoe box, or perhaps a bit larger. Collect some or all of the following to place inside it:

- The front section of an issue of the daily newspaper, enclosed in sturdy plastic wrapping

- A weekly newsmagazine

- Extra or duplicate family photos from the past year (those that aren't needed for albums)

- Any ephemera you may have about the past year's popular books and movies (such as a best-seller list or top 10 movie lists), and other cultural phenomena (clip these from magazines, and/or include any programs or tickets saved from events your family has attended)

- Maps and brochures from the past year's family trips

- Memorabilia about home, garden, and companion animals

- Photocopies of awards from school and camp

You may think of other personal and cultural items you might like to place in your family's time capsule in addition to those listed above. Just make sure not to use items you'll need or want any time soon, like original awards and report cards, or the last remaining photo of your departed cat. Finally, have everyone sit down and think of favorite books, movies, concerts, and plays, memorable outings and restaurant meals, and other events and accomplishments from the year just past. Have a designated list-maker note all these items (or have everyone make their own list), including any special anecdotes.

Seal the box and affix a note on it: "Do not open until . . ."

whatever date is mutually agreed upon. For younger children, even a year seems like a long time, but older children might agree to a waiting period of two to five years. Put the box in a safe spot. You need not bury it in the ground—stashing your time capsule in an attic or out-of-the-way closet is sufficient. If you start this tradition when your children are young, there will be a box to open each year and reminisce over, as you and your family put together the next time capsule.

Keep family stories alive with reunions: After her mother premature death, Stacie's aunts (her mother's sisters) felt a need to stay connected, and started to host yearly family reunions. After a few years, the aunts asked Stacie to hold the next reunion. Since she lives a few hours from where most of the family members live, she was afraid that no one would show up.

On the contrary, it was so well attended and so thoroughly enjoyed that Stacie has taken on the permanent task of hosting the reunions, and each year, the number of family members attending has grown. Stacie uses the reunion as a target date and incentive to get things spruced up and fixed around the house and garden; she noted that in a family that has suffered from rifts, the reunion helps heal estrangements.

Over the years, the extended family has established food and activity rituals that make things flow easily throughout this very intensive time together. Sports, skits, barbecues, Irish dance, and a bonfire are among the highlights; but no reunion would be the same without the usual family stories being told, enjoyed, and most important, kept alive.

The family reunion is a subject—indeed, a book—in and of itself. There's copious information on how to plan and host them — as well as various themes and approaches — at your fingertips on the internet. If the idea of reunions seems intriguing, yet daunting, there are many ways to "work up" to them, and they don't necessarily have to involve every living relative you have in the world. You can focus on a certain group of cousins, or on a geographic area where a good number of relatives are clustered. To get started, try sending an "intention letter" or e-mail, to feel out who might be interested in participating in and helping to organize such an event.

Adoption day traditions: Families with adopted children often find simple yet sustaining ways to revisit "the day we got you." Lisa and her husband show each of their daughters, adopted from China, the video taken on the day their adoption became official. They refer to each girl's adoption day as their "anniversary." The girls absolutely love watching the video of their adoptive parents receiving them as babies; watching the video spurs the retelling of stories and memories of each adoption.

This simple ritual is rich enough, says Lisa, without the giving of gifts or a meal, as is customary at birthdays.

Family history on file: As keeper of family history, Reed wanted to share some of the things she knew with everyone else. "A few years ago, I went through old calendars, journals, and photo albums and collected significant dates and events. Some were family milestones, like the day we moved into a new house, or when a cousin got married. Others were just moments I wanted to remember—losing a first tooth, or a particularly fun winter day."

"I took index cards and wrote an event and its year on an index card for that date. Now, every so often, we look at the card for that day's date and talk about what happened in our family

on that date. I've also used them to write notes for lunch boxes."
Help your children grow a family tree: Having your children work on creating a family tree at designated family gatherings such as yearly reunions, Thanksgiving, or a regularly held extended family dinner can be a richly rewarding ritual, and another good way to keep family stories alive. Make sure that kids understand that putting a family tree together can be a somewhat lengthy process, rewarded by an understanding of the family's roots and stories. At gatherings, kids can "interview" relatives and gather the following information:

- Birthdate and place

- Date and place of marriage

- Ancestral information from older relatives on those who are departed, such as birthplace and date, date of death, where they grew up, and where they are buried

- Names, birth and death dates, where they were from, when they married, names of offspring

Many genealogical web sites are available; some are helpful, while others are only there for profit. If your kids want to use web-based information, make sure to investigate sites to help them determine whether they are legitimate and useful. Not surprisingly, software to aid in creating family genealogies is available, and you might want to help your kids decide if they'd like to take a technical route or a more hands-on approach.

How elaborate to make the family tree should be decided upon in advance. It can be as simple as a big pedigree chart on poster board showing names, dates, marriages, and offspring. Or it can be done as a scrapbook or binder, including pages or pockets for written histories, or family stories recorded as audio files.

Encourage your kids to capture family stories, as the tradition of keeping them alive orally is certainly on the wane. Hearing about childhoods past is always fascinating for kids; when they hear the old saw about how grandpa walked five miles to school in blinding snowstorms, they are more likely to savor the tale than roll their eyes if they are recording it for posterity.

Photos can also be included in a scrapbook-style family tree. Your kids can ask their aunts, uncles, and grandparents to donate pictures that they are willing to spare for the project, and affix them on appropriate pages. Current pictures that they themselves take can be included as well. If the process of putting together a family tree of any sort starts to outweigh the outcome or reward, consider creating a "family memory box" at a regularly attended event, such as Thanksgiving or the winter holidays, where everyone brings an item or two (dated photos, letters, birth certificates, etc.—photocopies are preferable).

The memory box can be "visited" and added to on each of these occasions. It may not be as formal as a family tree or memory album, but is still a simple and rewarding way to preserve family history and stories.

Honoring the Departed

In most modern cultures, there are rituals for burying departed loved ones, but few for honoring their memories. Yet rites for honoring ancestors and commemorating the departed are intrinsic to more traditional cultures all over the world.

- Mexico's Day of the Dead is one example. An elaborate yearly tradition, this joyous celebration encourages viewing death as part of the cycle of changes, not something frightening. Festivities include sugar sculptures of skulls and bones, special breads and other delicious ceremonial foods, colorful decorations, and candlelit midnight marches to graveyards.

- Samhain was the Celtic predecessor of today's Halloween, and has much in common with Mexican Day of the Dead. It was a day to celebrate the dead with food, drink, magic, and divination. Cait Johnson, in *Witch in the Kitchen,* writes of Samhain, "Today is the perfect day to set the table with those old plates or glasses that were left to you by your grandmother, your aunt, or your mother. . . . Set an extra place for anyone who died in the past year, or for a special relative or friend. Tell loving stories about them at dinner."

- Asian and African cultures have long held cherished rituals for honoring ancestors, who are believed to remain an integral presence in the family. The Korean New Year, for example, also serves as a day for honoring ancestors and strengthening family connections. A central rite of the day honors the past four generations of ancestors.

- In other parts of Asia, a special date is set aside as Respect for Ancestors Day. The day begins by leaving offerings of beautifully prepared foods and flowers at grave sites, and ends with a festive meal eaten at home, marking both a tribute to, and separation from the departed.

These ancestor-honoring rituals might be more readily admired than envied outside their cultures. Still, there are many simple ways we can commemorate loved ones once they've passed on.

Ancestor feast: Some families practice a symbolic ritual of remembrance to honor the departed on the anniversary of their birth or death. They set an extra plate at the table, complete with food, lit by a candle, and surrounded by several photos of the departed. Serve that person's favorite dishes, their signature recipes, or foods that reflect their cultural heritage. What were some of the special dishes they made that left a lasting impression on you?

Have your children help in selecting and preparing foods for this commemoration. The flavors and aromas associated with a relative's favorite foods are a concrete way to bring memories alive. And if not an entire meal, baking or cooking something just like Mom, Dad, or Grandma did can be just as effective a way to pass something of that person along to your own children.

Memorial altar: Consider creating a special altar on the person's birthday, with flowers, photos, and other memorabilia, as is done in some Eastern cultures. Place a special plate of food as an offering, perhaps special foods symbolizing those enjoyed by the person being honored. Tell stories and share memories about the departed.

If one of your or your partner's parents or grandparents is being honored, your children may especially enjoy finding out more about their ethnic backgrounds. Prepare a meal reflecting their cultural background; look at maps of the region, or a globe, to locate where they were born and grew up.

"Ancestral vessel": In some societies, vaselike containers were once fashioned to hold small worldly belongings of the departed. If you have small items that belonged to a departed loved one, consider making or purchasing a modern version of a "reliquary vessel." This can be a decorative box and used for storing small keepsakes that belonged to that person, such as watches and other jewelry, passports, coins, medals, awards, or other items that may have been part of their personal collection, plus some photos of or belonging to them.

Each year, on the anniversary of this person's birth or death, the container can be taken from its special place. The objects and photos can be laid out to admire, and reminisce over, keeping alive the unique story of the individual's life.

Plant a memory garden: Here's a lovely and lasting tribute. Plant a small garden in honor of the departed. Consider having a small tree, such as a Japanese maple or weeping cherry, as the centerpiece. Designate an annual ritual of adding something to the garden in the late spring or early summer of each year. If space allows, place a bench near this garden for sitting, meditating, and remembering.

Part Four
Seasonal Rites

"*Those who contemplate the beauty of the earth find reserves of strength that will endure as long as life lasts. There is symbolic as well as actual beauty in the migration of birds, the ebb and flow of the tides, the folded bud ready for the spring. There is something infinitely healing in the repeated refrains of nature — the assurance that dawn comes after night, and spring after the winter.*"

—Rachel Carson, *The Sense of Wonder*

When my younger son was in kindergarten, his class made a construction paper graph to determine which season was the kids' favorite. This took place in January. With less than a handful of exceptions, they all chose winter.

I was flabbergasted! While parents were grumbling about colds, flu, icy roads, and gloomy skies, these kids came up with all kinds of reasons why winter is wonderful (Christmas! Hanukkah! Snow angels! Skating!). It dawned on me that this since this project was done in midwinter, the children would naturally gravitate toward the present season as their favorite, since kids are so "in the moment." If the bar graph project had been done in any other season, that would likely be the one chosen as the hands-down favorite.

As we grow into adulthood, many of us lose touch with a natural connection to the seasons and the unique pleasures of each. Our culture gives us few reasons—or reminders—to live according to seasonal rhythms. It's odd that the most intense period of celebrating and socializing occurs right around the winter solstice, when darkness falls at an unreasonably early hour.

High spirits, frantic shopping, nonstop preparation, last-minute travel, and perpetual hubbub rule the human world just as all of nature and its creatures begin a period of dormancy. That post-holiday letdown many people experience may not be so much due to the holidays ending, but rather to fighting the natural inclination toward quiet and retreat during the darkest days of the year.

Conversely, many of us spend entire summers in climate-controlled offices when we should be lounging in hammocks, going on picnics, swimming, and socializing. I'm not sure what can be done about this—there's no movement, as far as I know, to move winter holidays to July, nor one that would allow those with full-time jobs to take entire summers off. In parts of the world down under, like Australia and New Zealand, Christmas is celebrated at the height of summer; in Europe, the long summer holiday is a fact of life.

Obstacles aside, it's entirely possible to reacquaint ourselves with the natural cycles of the year and celebrate the unique qualities of each season as it comes around. For those of us who are not too religious, celebrating the start of each season can offer an alternative to denominational rites.

Natural cycles impact on our physical, emotional, and psychological well-being. By just being more aware of the seasons, we regain our sense of wonder for them. Reinforcing your children's intuitive interest in seasonal changes is great motivation for heightening your own awareness.

When we honor the annual cycles of sprouting, growth, fruiting, decaying, and sprouting again, we give ourselves the gift of serenity. There is something deeply satisfying and reassuring about those cycles, a promise of birth and renewal while honoring the processes of death and decay. By consciously aligning ourselves with the pattern we honor our own processes — and we make a deep and powerful connection with our planet.

— Cait Johnson and Maura D. Shaw,
Celebrating the Great Mother

• • • • •

Nature Activities Through the Seasons

Observing the natural world keeps our sense of awe alive. Wonder comes in all sizes, from a graceful hummingbird or a spider spinning its web, to a solar eclipse or a desert canyon. If you haven't got the time or inclination for mountain biking or white-water rafting, and if the whole notion of "adventure vacations" is an oxymoron as far as you're concerned, fear not. The natural world can be enjoyed in a variety of small, tame doses.

Some children take to nature—well, naturally. Others balk and complain ("It's too buggy!" "I'm bored!" "My legs are tired!"). For the latter, especially, constructing enjoyable traditions around nature outings can be key to ensuring mutual enjoyment. A favorite, familiar place at which the children can enjoy predictable yet pleasurable activities helps ensure anticipation rather than angst.

- If you'd like your children to gain a greater appreciation for nature, try designing rituals around the following and other outdoor activities you already enjoy. Tie them into a special place or particular season; pack a picnic to help turn these outings into traditions:

- Most kids love to be on the water. Rent a boat, canoe, or kayak, and find out in advance what you can expect to observe, for example, a rookery (bird-hatching area). Teach your kids to take great care while visiting these ecologically sensitive areas.

- To add enticement to outdoor adventures, especially for younger children, play games such as scavenger hunt or "I spy." Bring items to sharpen the power of observation—sketchbooks (for quick sketches and leaf rubbings), disposable cameras, binoculars, and magnifying glasses. Guides to identify wildflowers, leaves, or wild mushrooms are enticing to older children.

- Go on an organized bird-watching expedition. See what child-friendly events your local Audubon Society sponsors each year. Or, participate in a hawk or eagle watch. Bird-related activities are year-round events. Log onto the Audubon Society to find a local chapter near you.

- Explore the teeming life of a pond or swamp in early spring; look for turtles, frogs, waterfowl and their young. Bring small nets and containers (fill them with water from the pond) to scoop out and observe animal life, but put everything right back afterwards.

- In midsummer, take a trip to a butterfly garden or conservatory. Make sure to give each child a guide to help them see how many varieties they can find.

- Visit a botanical garden or arboretum. Late spring is an especially good time, with flowering trees in bloom. Give children a map and assign each one to find specific plants or trees. Make this into a noncompetitive game, but do offer a reward of an ice cream or some other enticing small perk.

- Spring, summer, or fall are all good seasons for hiking to a waterfall or a modest summit, then taking in the view while enjoying a picnic. Make sure to bring some of the aforementioned tools—magnifying glasses, binoculars, and such, to make the journey more interesting for the young.

- Be backyard astronomers—make regular dates to observe the night sky. Subscribe to "Sky Tips," an e-newsletter provided by Star Date Online (www.StarDate.org); find out what to look for in the sky each month.

- In different locales, and at various times of the year, take your kids on a hunt for "nature's art supplies." Collect leaves, curly vines, seeds, and pinecones in autumn woods; search for smooth pebbles along rivers or streams; pick up seashells, driftwood, and sea glass along a shoreline. Use care and common sense to determine what can be collected and taken home. Once home, do art projects with your finds: leaf rubbings, pinecone swags, seed pictures, seashell necklaces, sea glass mosaics.

Spring planting traditions

Those of us in four-season climates have seen spring return dozens of times, yet it's impossible not to feel awed each time it arrives. Spring exemplifies hope, renewal, and possibility. As we emerge from winter's hibernation, our minds burst with new projects, plans, and ambitions.

An urge to clear, clean, and start anew takes over, making room to sow seeds, both literally and figuratively. These "seeds" are symbolic of creative ideas and desires that have yet to unfold and that, with luck, will flourish in the seasons ahead. Spring is the season to emerge, explore, feed the senses, and feel wonder.

Planting activities are metaphoric for the sense of renewal that each spring brings:

- On the first day of spring, have a seed-planting ceremony. Start seedlings indoors for container gardens or planting outdoors later in the season. Tomatoes, herbs, vegetables, and flowers all hold the possibility of summer pleasures. Miniature "greenhouse kits," available at garden centers, make the process easy and exciting. Or go the old-fashioned route with egg crates, potting soil, and judicious watering.

- Follow up by finding out the exact date in your region when it's safe to transfer young plants outdoors. Hold an annual planting day for the new plants sown from seed.

- Each year, create at least one festive garden project with a child, such as a container vegetable garden, a miniature desertscape, or a flowering window box. A splendid source for these and other easy garden projects is *My First Garden Book*.

- Take an annual outing to a park, arboretum, or botanical garden and let your eyes feast on flowering trees like cherry, dogwood, and magnolia. If you have access to these kinds of trees, such as on your own or a friend's property, carefully prune a few branches to bring indoors, and display them in a vase.

- Repot indoor plants that have become pot bound. Potted plants are often constrained after winter, and need more room to grow—just as we do after a winter spent mainly indoors.

- Create a festive centerpiece of budding branches of pussy willows, freesia, or forsythia. Surround these with one or more vases of daisies, lilies, and irises. Delicate, budlike flowers are always welcome, as are pots of flowering bulbs.

Springtime is perfect for picnics

A delicious meal eaten outdoors—deliberately planned, at any time of year—is a perfect springboard for creating tradition. One of my favorite warm-season rituals is seeking out wonderful new places to combine an outdoor adventure with a picnic. Fortunately, I live in a region that offers a life's supply of remarkable picnic spots.

It may have been sneaky, but when our kids were young, we always found that they were more enticed by nature outings if we called them "picnics" rather than "hikes." Now that our sons are older, and immune to such subterfuge, the pleasure of returning to a well-loved place and following a familiar routine with well-stocked knapsacks has not lost its charm.

"A picnic is rather like a dream, if you pick your spot, your companions, and your food. You can make it as simple or elaborate as you want."

— Laurie Colwin, *More Home Cooking*

Sue shared an offbeat story of a family picnic tradition. From the time she was about seven years old, her parents and siblings had weekly "opposite season" picnics at a public lake about an hour from their Michigan home, no matter what the weather. Most vivid in her memory are -images of the family tromping through snow, wind, and rain, doing a "wood hunt" for dried twigs with which to start a fire in the barbecue pit.

After a fire-roasted lunch, they did some sort of physical activity—a long walk, if weather permitted; skating or sledding in the winter. The weekly picnic continued until Sue was in her mid-thirties, with two children of her own, allowing regular, anticipated time for her parents to connect with their grandkids. Once her parents moved to California, the ritual ended, since they'd been the driving force behind it. The cold-weather picnics are among Sue's fondest childhood memories, and she hopes her own children, now grown as well, share the feeling.

Here's some more inspiration, to start some picnic traditions of your own:

- Some picnic adventures are invigorating, others are relaxing and meditative. One of our favorite places is a Buddhist monastery with pagoda-like structures set among simple gardens and ponds. The monastery welcomes picnickers, but cautions that "vegetarian rules apply." Buddhist monasteries and other contemplative retreats can be found in the most surprising of areas; see if there's one near you, and inquire in advance if they welcome day visitors.

- State and national landmarks are also fun, combining a good outdoor meal with a gentle lesson in history. Nearby, the Hudson River is lined with the mansions and gardens

of nineteenth-century industrialists and political figures
like the Vanderbilts and Roosevelts. Now open to the public, these venues welcome visitors and their picnic supplies.
Do a little -research on historic sites in your area. Many
welcome visitors bearing food by offering designated picnic
areas; often, these sites also have lovely gardens or trails to
explore as well.

- A hike at a nature preserve is sure to whet the appetite. For
  some, nothing appeals more than a picnic at a beach. For
  more sophisticated tastes or when picnicking with a special
  sweetheart, have your outdoor meal with an open air concert. River banks, waterfalls, arboretums, and even beautifully landscaped college campuses offer sensory pleasures
  lasting long after the last morsel is consumed.

- For families with young children, an ideal spot for a casual
  picnic with little ones is a community park, combined with
  a visit to a great playground. Similarly, combining a lake
  shore picnic with swimming, boating, or kite flying makes
  the experience more appealing to younger kids.

- While spring may be the perfect time for a picnic ritual,
  heralding as it does the arrival of warm season pleasures,
  autumn is also a splendid time for combining picnics with
  hikes, and not just for the obvious enjoyment of the splendid colors. The slight chill in the air is perfectly suited to a
  hiker's gear and garb. And the shifting quality of autumn's
  light—suddenly more shadowy than summer's warm
  glow—is an urgent reminder to savor what's left before
  those shorter days set in.

As for the food: For some, a picnic is mainly about the food, but not for me. I can recall every exquisite place where I've enjoyed an outdoor meal, but I'd be hard pressed to tell you what I ate. A picnic can be just as blissful with sandwiches and juice as with fancier fare and wine. I like to think of the food as parallel to the experience itself: Simple, healthy, and unpretentious.

- The meal should be easy to serve and taste good at room temperature. Light dishes that provide quick energy to sustain a walk, hike, or swim are the cornerstones of a wholesome picnic menu. A too-heavy meal might put you more in the mood for a nap than for activity!

- Over the years, I've developed a formula of sorts for the meal, so it's easy for me to pack a picnic, even on the spur of a moment: Start with a good bread and a tasty spread (packed separately in a container); add two hearty salads (potato salad is always welcome, as are grain salads). Finish with fresh fruit (washed ahead of time and packed into containers), an optional dessert (nothing gooey that will be likely to melt!), and plenty of beverages.

- If your picnic plans are too last-minute to make even a simple meal, consider buying an assortment of good-quality prepared salads, spreads, and relishes at a deli counter or specialty grocery. Treat yourself to a meal with a theme, such as Middle Eastern: store-bought hummus, fresh pita bread, cured olives, stuffed grape leaves, and tabouleh salad are perfect for a fuss-free outdoor meal.

A picnic as fine a form of relaxation and renewal with a family in tow as it is when it's a romantic date with your significant other — whether at beaches, waterfalls, national historic landmarks, or botanic gardens. A lovely vista, some not-too-rigorous physical activity, and simple, tasty fare are the prime ingredients for a perfect picnic. Making them a regular part of seasonal forays, and returning to favorite places helps elevate picnics to ritual status. The experience is transformed from merely eating lunch outdoors to a refreshing lift for the spirit and senses.

Summer relaxation rituals

In many Asian traditions, summer's symbolic element, not surprisingly, is fire. The gradual awakening of spring segues (sometimes too quickly) into a period of heat and radiance. Summer's fiery energy is expansive—it invites you to play, enjoy friends, travel.

The world around us is zesty, delicious, and abundant. Blossoming gives way to ripening. As the fruits of the earth ripen, so can the dreams and projects that started as seeds in the spring. See if you can nurture what you've sown, both literally and figuratively.

- Have an annual family campout, even if it's in your own back yard. Have a campfire, and set up tents. Enjoy a cookout, then stay up late telling stories and stargazing.

- Set up pots of fresh herbs in a sunny windowsill, or on a porch or deck. If you prefer not to grow your own, make sure to buy fragrant bunches at farm markets to embellish summer fare.

- Make a tradition of deliberately choosing to learn something new each summer. Brush up on foreign languages or your family's favorite periods in history; read political or literary biographies at a shared reading level; or tackle a new craft or skill.

- Have a yearly ceremony of changing your home decor: Cover your sofas with cotton slipcovers, and your beds with cool cotton sheets and blankets. Place lots of bright flowers in every available vase, in every room of the house.

- Summer food traditions include fresh corn on the cob, berries, melons, and other luscious fruits, tomatoes, and more tomatoes! Feed your palate's preference for minimally cooked, light foods with cold soups, veggie-filled wraps, and bountiful salads. Wash it all down with homemade lemonade, and top it off with ice cream.

- During any beach visits, collect sea glass, shells, pebbles, and driftwood. Do art projects with your children from your finds—sea glass mosaics, shell-covered picture frames, or driftwood mobiles.

- At the end of summer, make a simple memory book of the summer's activities and adventures. During the course of the summer, save memorabilia in a box—camp and vacation pictures, ticket stubs, travel brochures, postcards, and other paraphernalia. Use a quiet, rainy morning to glue them into a sturdy blank journal.

Beach traditions, local outings, and vacations at home: Some of the most evocative childhood memories are made of sand and sun. Somehow, time spent at the beach becomes a cherished tradition for those lucky enough to have access to a shoreline. Carolyn has been going to Cape Cod nearly every summer since she was a child, and has been taking her daughter, Chelsea, there for at least one week each summer to enjoy the same things she did when she was young.

They bike into town or take the path to Provincetown, go on a whale watch and to the Audubon Society, and walk on their favorite rocky beach. The warm bays and ponds, the beauty of the light and colors, and the air's briny scent add up to a cherished tradition that Carolyn can't imagine doing without, even but for one week each summer. At the age of fourteen, Chelsea already appreciates the lure of the familiar, and can envision continuing the ritual into her own adulthood.

Beth's family enjoys an enviable week-long mini-reunion at the end of each summer—six side-by-side cottages on the Jersey Shore for her family, and the families of her two sisters, her husband's brother, and each set of their parents. The days consist of cousins playing together, parents relaxing together, cooperatively made barbecue dinners, and lots of reading.

Traditional summer outings: Having at least one must-do summer outing—something old-fashioned, bordering on corny—can make the season complete. You probably already have a favorite summer activity or two. Elevate them to the status of tradition and see how much more satisfying they can be. Consider your family's preferences and interests; try a few of these outings on for size. Decide whether your special outing traditions will be solely for your own family, or a chance to join forces with another family. Here are a few possibilities:

- Attend one major league baseball game.

- Go to an old-fashioned country fair.

- Ferry to an island for a picnic.

- Take a long, leisurely bicycle ride on a favorite trail.

- Attend an outdoor theater performance, concert, or Shakespeare festival.

Be a tourist in your own town: Adventure trips are good, taking you out of your comfort zone, though admittedly, they are work (the word travel is derived from the French *travaille*, which in fact, means work). Families with young children, lots of children, or those who simply can't get away in the summer might enjoy a tradition of being "tourists" at home.

Designate a day each week, or a long weekend, to visit places you never seem to get to when you're in work-and-school mode, such as museums, historic sites, and recreational areas. Eat dinner at new or favorite restaurants, get tickets to summer stock theater or an outdoor concert. Pack a picnic for lunch and explore an out-of-the-way waterfall; take a tour by bicycle; hop on a train or ferry to poke around a neighboring town that you never seem to get around to visiting.

Rituals for Our Times authors Evan Imber-Black and Janine Roberts describe a family that plans a "vacation at home" each year. This family of six found that they came back from their vacations exhausted and feeling that they had spent too much money. Instead, they began spending a yearly vacation at home.

They prepared favorite foods ahead of time, ate out more than usual, and made a commitment to put off chores, turn off the phone, and limit TV. Each day they did a nearby activity that they all looked forward to. Getting into vacation mode while at home does take a certain amount of discipline, but is an effort worth making when going further afield is not an option. Packing the day with local activities that you rarely get around to, and ending up in your own beds, can be perfectly blissful.

Fall festivities

In Chinese tradition, the earth's energy is said to begin pulling inward and contracting. Fall brings conflicting emotions: On one hand, it's somewhat dispiriting when darkness falls at 5:00 by the end of October, with only shorter, colder days to look forward to for some time. On the other hand, nippy air can be so welcome following summer's heat.

Parents feel mixed emotions as their children return to school — we miss their presence and the open days of summer, yet it's nice to have more time for ourselves. Fall's themes of harvest or gathering can be applied to our personal endeavors. Like gathering the season's abundant crops, we can also reap what has blossomed in our lives throughout the year.

- If you're lucky enough to have a fireplace in your home, make the first one of the season a special occasion. Make a hearty seasonal stew, or pumpkin bread and cider to enjoy before a roaring fire. Cait Johnson, in *Celebrating the Great Mother*, writes that she throws a handful of sea salt and a couple of bay leaves into the season's first fire as symbols of protection.

- An early fall "moon viewing party" has long been a tradition in Japan. Each September, shrines and other community organizations celebrate Kangetsu-sai to celebrate the beauty of the harvest moon with traditional music, dancing, poetry, and blessings. Have your own "moon viewing" ritual by taking autumn walks in the light of the full moon.

- Celebrate leaves! Go on an annual "leaf-peeping" expedition, following a familiar route to observe the changing landscape. Collect colorful leaves and press them in heavy books between sheets of waxed paper. Have your kids make leaf rubbings. Make a leaf pile for your children to jump into; jump into it yourself!

- Each fall, make a date with your family to plant lots of bulbs for perennials that will emerge the following spring. Show children pictures of what they can expect to pop out of the ground after the snow melts.

- Decorate your home with farm stand finds: Use pumpkins, squashes, Indian corn, gourds, and fall flowers like mums and asters to make arrangements in your kitchen, on your porch, and indeed any place in your home that would benefit from these predictable, yet perennially pleasing arrangements.

- Prepare jars of grains, dried beans, whole-grain flours, dried fruits, nuts, and seeds. Just as the animal world performs its annual rite of putting away stores of food for the coming colder months, you too can enjoy a wholesome annual ritual of gathering and storing. For this, I use quart-sized mason jars, available by the case in any hardware or agricultural supply store. I also display them prominently on my kitchen shelves, as a reminder to use these nourishing foods as often as possible.

- Late fall is pumpkin season. Take your kids to a pumpkin patch and select sugar pumpkins for baking pies, making soups and stews, and incorporating into sweet quick breads and muffins. Choose large pumpkins for jack-o-lanterns or for simply setting at your doorstep. Enjoy hot apple cider with fresh pumpkin bread. Attend an autumn harvest or pumpkin festival. They often pair seasonal food and wonderful music, backdropped by dazzling foliage.

Warming winter traditions

Winter's themes are dormancy and regeneration. By honoring rather than fighting this quieter part of the natural cycle, you'll be ever more ready for the blossoming of spring. Unless you're the type who begins waxing her skis as soon as the first snowflake falls, the ideal antidote to winter's chill and gloom is to turn inward and give in to the natural tendency to retreat.

Instead of feeling frustrated by the cold, dark period from January to March, try to savor a slower pace, and incorporate more deliberate solitude and quiet time into your days. Teach your children to do the same. It can be a delightful time to retreat to the shelter of home and hearth and get things done without the distractions afforded by the other seasons. Direct your focus inward to stay in balance, and break the season's monotony with fun, comforting treats.

- If a snowstorm is headed your way, prepare for a relaxing snow day with a 1000- or 1500-piece jigsaw puzzle, some good-quality cocoa for making hot chocolate, a few entertaining videos and good books, and plenty of wood, if you have a fireplace or wood stove.

- Stop fighting the snow and have some fun with it—go sledding, snow shoeing, or cross-country skiing; take a walk in the silence of winter woods. Do corny snow activities with your partner or kids—make snowmen, snow angels, snow ice cream.

- Put up nesting boxes and bird feeders for wintering birds. You'll be astonished at the number of birds that remain in cold areas for the winter, and at the amount of pleasure gained from observing them. You'll find everything you need to know about feeding and sheltering wintering birds at the Cornell Lab of Ornithology, http://www.birds.cornell.edu/programs/AllAboutBirds/AttractingBirds/FeedingBirds/FeedPestsPredators.html

- Have staples on hand to cook comforting soups and stews all season. To create a soup tradition, have a weekly "soup and bread night" all winter. Make sure you have your favorite seasonings on hand—an all-purpose seasoning mix, good-quality curry powder, an Italian seasoning blend are among those I find indispensable. Add good pot and ladle, and attractive soup bowls or crocks.

115

- Many of us approach winter solstice—the shortest day of the year— with dread. On the flip side, though, the day marks the beginning of light returning as the sun starts moving northward again. Winter solstice is part of the ancient tradition of Yule, celebrated December 20 to 23. Many people like to use this time to decorate their Christmas tree and put up lots of lights. Others fill their homes with lit candles, build a bonfire, or sing and tell stories about the sun.

Winter "cabin fever" fun

If you have preschoolers or young school-age children home on snow days and sick days, creating special "cabin fever" rituals will help you actually look forward to, rather than dread, those long days at home.

Some parents told me of a "cabin fever" drawer filled with special games, toys, and treats that come out only on these occasions, lending an otherwise gloomy day a festive air. When my children were young, snow days would mean pulling out a favorite "kitchen chemistry" book. They'd be excited and occupied experimenting with baking soda and vinegar, cornstarch and water, and other experiments.

Several cold, homebound days in a row can be challenging for parents of young children, but activities specifically designated for these kinds of days can make them feel more like a cozy retreat. Here are some simple ideas:

- On a dismal February day, plan a festive indoor picnic. Take a break from the predictable comfort foods of the season and have the kids help prepare an array of light finger foods, sandwiches, potato salad, and lemonade. Spread a blanket and, if possible, have the picnic before a cheering fire.

- Similarly, plan an annual indoor camping trip just when everyone has really had it with winter, or be ready to have one when a snowstorm is predicted. Borrow a few beautifully photographed books on national parks or other natural wonders from the library. Decide where you are "going" for your trip by browsing through the books (and in the process, learning about some amazing places). Bring out the sleeping bags and air mattresses; pitch a small pup tent if you have one. Plan a cookout-style meal and tell great stories around a "campfire" (a real roaring fire in your fireplace, or an imagined campfire).

  Use flashlights instead of incandescent lights. Have everyone sleep in the living room or family room. This winter spirit-lifter can be great fun even for those who don't care for real camping trips!

- Prepare a box of letter-writing supplies especially for these kinds of stay-at-home days. Have the kids make beautiful cards using collage materials, stamp kits, stickers, and scented markers. Craft stores are a good source for blank cards and the aforementioned supplies. Once the cards are made, have the children write letters and notes to distant relatives and friends. Make a ceremony out of taking all the mail to the post office. The fun is extended if the kids start getting replies via snail mail!

- Just before the winter holidays begin, visit a local thrift shop and stock up on dress-up clothes. Around the time of the holidays, these shops tend to have fancier and more offbeat items that are perfect for this sort of endeavor. Make sure to include accessories like scarves, belts, and hats. After the clothes are cleaned, find a special container for them, like a wicker laundry basket or a toy chest. Take it out on a day when the winter blues descend, and watch the fun begin. Let the kids do what kids do best and just pretend, or encourage them to make up skits.

- When my kids were young and cabin fever hit hard, I always turned to the one indoor activity that never seemed to lose its charm—baking projects. Homemade cookies, muffins, and quick breads go a long way toward brightening days when you feel that winter will never end. If you are a bit more ambitious, cabin fever days are the perfect occasions to try the long, slow process of making yeasted breads with your kids. Enjoying warm, wholesome treats fresh from the oven nourishes body, soul, and senses at once.

Resources

Celebrating the Great Mother: A Handbook of Earth-Honoring Activities for Parents and Children by Cait Johnson and Maura D. Shaw. This book is a fantastic resource for earth-centered seasonal celebrations. These include solstices, equinoxes, Yule, Ostara, Beltane, and others, with crafts, activities, blessings, meditations, and more, all geared to families with young and older children.

Cracked Corn and Snow Ice Cream: A Family Almanac by Nancy Willard. This beautifully designed and illustrated country almanac takes the reader through the year with significant dates, bucolic lore, projects, and recipes.

Nature's Art Box: From T-Shirts to Twig Baskets, 65 Cool Projects for Crafty Kids to Make with Natural Materials You Can Find Anywhere by Laura C. Martin. If you're trying to tempt your kids to venture into the natural world, this book provides ample incentive.

Nature in a Nutshell for Kids: Over 100 Activities You Can Do in Ten Minutes or Less by Jean Potter. Same comment as the one above—another fun resource.

Cooking Art: Easy Edible Art for Young Children by MaryAnn F. Kohl and Jean Potter is an adorable book filled with simple and rewarding cooking projects to do with little ones, great for "cabin fever" diversions.

In Conclusion: Thinking About Your Own
Rituals and Traditions

Hopefully, this book has given you much to ponder, many ideas, and inspiration for rituals and traditions that elevate ordinary living. Finally, though, what makes a ritual work is that you've made it your own.

Not that it has to be completely unique or creative, but that it's just right for you and your family. Use these pages ponder the rituals you already enjoy, think about ways to tweak your routines into rituals, and muse about rituals and traditions you'd like to establish.

Personal rituals: What, when, and how often?

Your first step in recording and refining your rituals is to simply inventory them. Write your existing rituals as well as "almost-ritual" routines — make a simple "laundry list." This will give you a better idea of the things you do regularly. You can use a physical notebook or a text document on your computer to begin your wish list of rituals you'd like to establish, or at least try on for size.

As you think about the various kinds of rituals and traditions you and your family and friends already enjoy or want to try, remember that there are many things we do on a regular basis that feel more like routines, because we haven't given them much thought.

Certain routines, like brushing your teeth or taking out the garbage, need to stay in the routine category. Others, though, can be elevated into ritual by giving them attention and some added flourish. What ordinary activities would you like to transform into rituals? Making and eating daily dinner, getting together with a particular group of friends, reading books, going for walks, or even going to sleep can be given just enough personal flair to become rituals.

Daily rituals: Include here rituals for mealtimes, hellos, goodbyes, good mornings, good nights, private time—anything you do on a daily basis. Don't worry if this one's a short list—no one can be expected to have lots of daily rituals.

Weekly rituals: Think about what you do to celebrate the end of a busy week or what you do for regular family fun. Do you have a family meeting, participate in regular volunteer activities, or shared physical activities?

Monthly rituals: Do you get together with your friends once a month for a specific purpose, like a book club or knitting group? Do you have a one-on-one evening out with one of your children? Does your family do a once-a-month outing to a nearby city, park, or museum?

Seasonal rituals: Are there particular activities your family enjoys or would enjoy doing each spring, summer, winter, and fall? Is there a vacation spot you return to each year, at a particular time of year? Are there nature activities you are drawn to doing each season? Do you acknowledge the winter or summer solstice?

Yearly rituals: Into this category fall birthdays, anniversaries and other celebrations, the big annual vacation, reunions, and such. You can also include offbeat things like celebrating Groundhog Day, attending the county fair, or participating in an annual walkathon—anything that happens mainly once a year, but that has significance in your family's repertoire.

Holiday and special celebration rituals: We didn't spend a lot of time on traditional holiday rituals in this book. Still, since you're already thinking about your rituals, take time to record your favorite holiday traditions. While doing so, you may even think of ways to make them better.

Food rituals and traditions: Many rituals, ordinary or celebratory, involve food. What food rituals are important to you? Are there particular seasonal foods you enjoy? Do you shop at an offbeat market each week? What are your family's favorite comfort foods? Do you have a "cooking together" ritual with family members or friends? Do you gather for regular meals with extended family, or participate in a dinner club?

Rituals of remembrance: What rituals do you have in place that preserve your family's unique story? How do you celebrate milestones, rites of passage, "first and lasts" (such as the first day of a new grade, or the last day of soccer season) so that they will be remembered? Do you have a special way to record your children's growth and milestones, like a scrapbook, or a wall of photos that are taken in the same spot each year? Do you honor departed loved ones, or hold reunions to keep family stories alive?

Letting go of rituals: Sometimes, rituals reach their natural conclusion. A child no longer wants you to read to them at night (they'd rather lose themselves in chapter books); a combination Sunday brunch and family meeting dwindles with your teen's need to sleep late; your child no longer wants to bake with you on Saturday mornings, preferring instead to take karate or skateboard with friends.

There's no set way to let go of rituals, except with grace, and with the acceptance that it's no longer a ritual once it feels more like an obligation. Sometimes, it helps to simply acknowledge that the ritual has reached its natural conclusion, and to put into words what was most enjoyable about it while it lasted. Consider what they meant to you and/or your family, and how you felt when it was time to let them go.

About the Editor

Jordan St. Clair-Jackson enjoys writing about food, health, lifestyle, and culture. She's a longtime contributor to VegKitchen and other websites, and is the author of *Maca Root for Health and Vitality; Healthy School Lunch;* and other titles.

Lightning Source UK Ltd.
Milton Keynes UK
UKHW021840021218
333357UK00023B/877/P

9 781540 549846